Alive in the Spirit!

Alive in the Spirit!

Confirmation Preparation for Young People

Leader's Guide

Catherine Ecker

Margaret Bick

NOVALIS

LTP
LITURGY
TRAINING
PUBLICATIONS

© 2006 Novalis, Saint Paul University, Ottawa, Canada

LITURGY
TRAINING
PUBLICATIONS

Editor: Patrick Gallagher
Cover: Anna Payne-Krzyzanowski
Layout: Anna Payne-Krzyzanowski

"Who Calls You by Name" by David Haas.
Copyright © 1988 by GIA Publications, Inc., 7404 S. Mason Ave.,
Chicago, IL 60638 www.giamusic.com 800.442.1358
All rights reserved. Used by permission.

Business Office:
Novalis
10 Lower Spadina Avenue, Suite 400
Toronto, ON
M5V 2Z2

Phone: 1-800-387-7164 or 416-363-3303 ext.239
Fax: 1-800-204-4140 or 416-363-9409
E-mail: resources@novalis.ca
www.novalis.ca

All rights reserved. No part of this publication
may be reproduced, stored in a retrieval system,
or transmitted in any form, or by any means,
electronic, mechanical, photocopying, recording,
or otherwise, without the written permission of the
publisher.

We acknowledge the financial support of the
Government of Canada through the Book
Publishing Industry Development Program
(BPIDP) for our publishing activities.

ISBN: 2-89507-610-3 (Novalis)
Printed in Canada.

Nihil Obstat
Reverend Louis J. Cameli, S.T.D.
Censor Deputatus
January 4, 2006

Imprimatur
Bishop-elect George J. Rassas
Vicar General
Archdiocese of Chicago
January 11, 2006

*The **Nihil Obstat** and **Imprimatur** are official declarations that a book
is free of doctrinal and moral error. No implication is contained therein
that those who have granted the **Nihil Obstat** and **Imprimatur** agree
with the content, opinions, or statements expressed. Nor do they assume
any legal responsibility associated with publication.*

Published in the United Stated of America by
Liturgy Training Publications,
1800 North Hermitage Avenue,
Chicago IL 60622-1101;
1-800-933-1800,
fax 1-800-933-7094,
email orders@ltp.org.
See our website at www.ltp.org.

Alive in the Spirit!: Confirmation Preparation for Young People,
Leader's Guide
ISBN 10: 1-56854-604-1 (Liturgy Training Publications)
ISBN 13: 978-1-56854-604-9 (Liturgy Training Publications)
AISCPL

Acknowledgments

We would very much like to thank the following reviewers for their valuable contribution to the development of this program:
Char Deslippe, Religious Education Coordinator, Diocese of Victoria, BC • Sr. Mary-Ann Bates, Diocesan Director of Catechetics, Diocese
of Prince George, BC • Sr. Gertrude Mulholland, Our Lady of Perpetual Help Parish, Sherwood Park, AB • Susan Suttie, Religious Education
Consultant, Diocese of Calgary, AB • Sr. Lorraine Couture, Catechetics Coordinator, Rural Catechetics Office, Prince Albert, SK • Agnes Rolheiser,
Rural Catechetics, Diocese of Saskatoon, SK • Carol Anne Seed, Director of Catechetics and Faith Formation, Archdiocese of Winnipeg, MB
Fr. Murray Kroetsch, Saint Pius X Church, Brantford, ON • Emily Di Fruscia, Assistant Director, Archdiocesan Office for Faith Formation, Montreal,
QC • Paul Toner, Director of Liturgy, Archdiocese of Moncton, Dieppe, NB • Madelyn Ramier, Diocesan Director of Catechetics, Diocese of
Saint John, Fredericton, NB • Marilyn Sweet, Director of Programs, Archdiocese of Halifax, NS • Margaret Craddock, Archdiocesan Director of
Catechesis, Archdiocese of St. John's, NL •

5 4 3 2 1   10 09 08 07 06

Table of Contents:

Welcome!

First, we want to thank you for your work in the Church. You have answered the call of God and the Church to share your faith with young Christians. We offer this program to help you. *Alive in the Spirit!* is different from most confirmation preparation programs in two important ways:
- its theological orientation
- its catechetical method.

Theological orientation

You may be accustomed to using confirmation preparation programs that treat the sacrament as a sacrament of Christian maturity, of taking responsibility for adult Christian life, of saying yes to baptism because an infant is not able to make baptismal vows. This may be the approach that was used when you were confirmed. Although this perspective does partially address the effect of the sacrament of confirmation in the life of the Christian, it focuses too much on the attitudes, actions and aptitudes of the candidate.

The approach to sacraments that underlies *Alive in the Spirit!* is that sacraments first and foremost reveal the action of God in the life of the candidate, not the other way around. The program invites candidates to grow increasingly attuned to the call God has made to them since the day of their baptism. It also invites them to come to the sacrament asking for divine help when they answer the baptismal call to live their lives at the table of the Lord and to be Christ in the world. It assumes they will continue to grow spiritually throughout their lives.

Confirmation is the second of the sacraments of initiation (baptism, confirmation and eucharist). In the sacraments of initiation a person is conformed to Christ, made one with him, made to be like him. In baptism we share in Christ's dying and rising; in confirmation we share in his exaltation as Spirit-filled Lord of glory; in eucharist we celebrate with him at the table of the Lamb of God, a foretaste of the heavenly banquet.

In order for the candidates to understand confirmation, this program looks first to the call of baptism. With an understanding of what God has done for us in baptism, we can reflect on the character of life after baptism, life in the family of God, life in the Christian community. The sacrament of confirmation reveals God's action of giving candidates the gift of the Holy Spirit for the life to which they are called in the sacrament of baptism: life at the eucharistic table and in the world.

That is why the foundation and starting point of this program is the action of

God in baptism. Because sacraments are about actions rather than things, *Alive in the Spirit!* describes the sacramental signs as actions rather than things, i.e., water bath rather than water, anointing rather than oil, clothing rather than a garment, enlightenment rather than a candle. Materials used in sacramental celebrations – water, oil, light, etc. – allow for layers of meaning. Describing the signs in terms of actions helps to focus on those layers of meaning the Church wishes to evoke in its rites.

Each session of the program explores one of the ritual actions in the celebration of baptism: the water bath, the anointing with chrism, the clothing in a baptismal garment, the presentation of a lighted candle, and the "ephphetha" (the opening of ears and mouth). The Church calls the latter four "explanatory rites"; although not necessary for validity, they reveal dimensions of the sacrament not immediately apparent in the water ritual.

Catechetical method

One of the most important tasks of growing up is making sense of the world. Young people are constantly finding meaning in everything around them and in everything that happens. Two of the tasks of those who mentor them are to help them interpret the world in a way that will be life-giving and to equip them to live full, happy, meaningful and productive lives. With that in mind, this program requires adults to:

* trust the power of ritual to communicate meaning
* trust the innate interpretive ability of young people
* help the candidates use the Church's perspective in their interpretation of the sacramental signs.

The strategy used in *Alive in the Spirit!* is based on the practice of the early Church called *mystagogia*, the interpretation of mystery. For early Christians, mystery was a synonym for sacrament. Only *after* the celebration of the sacraments of initiation did the bishop gather with the newly initiated to help them unfold the meaning of what they had experienced in the sacraments of baptism, confirmation and eucharist. To guide the new Christians to the implications of the sacramental signs he would

* gently remind them of each step in the ritual
* evoke the sensory experience
* draw on metaphor and theology.

Few of the candidates will have any first-hand memory of their baptism. Most will have heard something about the water bath; a few will still have their baptismal candle or their baptismal garment (or photos) tucked away in a safe place. All the sessions of this program begin with a ritual designed to provide an experience somewhat similar to one of the actions of the baptismal rite:

- exploring the qualities of water
- rubbing oil on the hands
- clothing oneself with Christ (special clothing and the cross)
- receiving a lit candle
- opening the mouth and ears (signing each with the sign of the cross).

Each session moves from a reflection on the sensory experience of the ritual to catechesis based on that experience. Following the experience and recollection, catechesis proceeds in several phases:

- from sensory experience to hints about God
- from God communicating by means of the ritual action to reasons for the use of that action in baptism
- from the intent of baptism to *my* life in the Christian community.

The final phase, under the heading "Connecting with Confirmation and Eucharist," addresses the way confirmation reveals how God will help me to live my life in the Christian community. This catechesis will deal with elements of the confirmation ritual, aspects of Christian life, the role of the gifts of the Holy Spirit, and the meaning of dining at the eucharistic table.

Preparing to use *Alive in the Spirit!*

Because *Alive in the Spirit!* is unlike most confirmation preparation programs, at first you may need to put a little extra energy into preparing to use it. Of course, you will be increasingly more comfortable the more you become familiar with the text and the flow of the sessions. But we have three suggestions to make your work easier.

Lay aside concerns

First, lay aside any concerns about the candidates' mastery of additional doctrinal content. Doctrinal content is for the religious education program. *Alive in the Spirit!* is experiential and is concerned with the candidates turning their whole being toward the loving God who made them and wishes to share life with them. The activities in their book are meant to continue their reflection on the sacramental signs and to help them sharpen their ability to tune into the broader language of the liturgy that shapes their lives.

Trust the method

Second, trust the method. The best way to come to an attitude of trust in the mystagogical method is to try it. Gather with other catechists (invite the parish clergy, too) to do one or more of the sessions among yourselves. If the number of catechists is small, invite some parishioners to join you. The Church uses simple "stuff" – actions with water, oil, candles, clothing – in its rituals precisely because of their power to allow God to speak. Remember, God used flesh and blood in Jesus Christ to speak God's ultimate word to humanity. Because God imbued creation with the power to speak of the divine, liturgy is able to transform the Sunday assembly for its life in the world. For this reason the signs are also able to speak to people of all ages.

Trust the candidates

Third, trust the candidates. Young people are truly engaged with their world and are natural interpreters and natural sign-makers. For example, they are experts at interpreting changes in nature, the beat of music, and the expressions on the faces of their friends and adults. Too often adults can look for "church" language and miss the language of the day that reflects a young person's vibrant faith. Young people seek an authentic relationship with God and are adept at participating in rituals in a safe and accepting environment. It is important that you believe in their desire to participate and are willing to reflect this belief back to them.

Trust in the ancient method, trust the

candidates, and witness the wisdom of the younger generation.

Introduction to Confirmation

The more you work with confirmation candidates, the more aware you will become that confirmation is the subject of much discussion today. You may already know that confirmation is celebrated with candidates of various ages depending on their home diocese. Some bishops now celebrate the sacrament of confirmation with children at the time of their first communion. In order to understand all this variety, it is helpful to know a bit about the history of confirmation and the role it has played in the lives of Christians.

Early confirmation practice

Written documents surviving from as early as the third century indicate that in the early Church no distinction was made between adults, children and infants at the time of Christian initiation. Everyone was baptized, confirmed and received communion in one celebration

– infants sharing only from the blood of Christ, by having a few drops applied to their lips or sucked from an adult finger.

Changing confirmation practice

The rapid growth of the Church soon posed a problem. The bishop could not be everywhere for the Easter Vigil, the customary time for initiation. So who would administer these sacraments? The Church in the eastern half of the Roman Empire decided that a priest could administer all these sacraments and the bishop's role would be to consecrate the chrism (this is their practice to this day). The Church of Rome (in the western half of the empire) decided that a priest could baptize, but candidates would have to wait for the bishop's visit in order to be confirmed and admitted to the eucharistic table. Although the separation in time between the sacraments was at first only a few days or weeks, eventually the time between baptism and the other two sacraments became years. But even with this long interval confirmation still came before first communion.

As years passed the reasons for the separation of the sacraments were forgotten. We began to attribute the delay in receiving the other two sacraments of initiation to a lack of knowledge and to social and even physical immaturity among the young candidates. In popular understanding, the delay took on a central role in our understanding of the sacrament, and confirmation became a time for concentrated religious education.

By 1910 few lay people were receiving communion at Mass. So Pope Pius X took measures to remedy this situation. One of these measures was to lower the age for first communion to "the age of reason" – now understood as the seventh year of life. Pius X made this change hoping that people would develop the habit of receiving communion regularly from an early age. Unfortunately, this change was implemented in different ways around the world. In some areas, such as most of North America, confirmation was not moved along with first communion, so in these places the sequence of the sacraments was disrupted. Although listed in canonical documents as the second sacrament of initiation, after 1910 confirmation was celebrated last in most of North America. However, in our multicultural society it is not difficult to find people who were confirmed elsewhere at a young age; there are probably several in your own parish.

Modern confirmation practice

Energetic liturgical and historical work since the Second Vatican Council of the mid-1960s has helped the Church gain a better understanding of how confirmation fits into the group of sacraments known as the sacraments of initiation. The Church now appreciates the importance of restoring confirmation to its proper place in the sequence of these sacraments.

The three sacraments of initiation – baptism, confirmation, eucharist – forever retain a bond. Out of a desire to make this bond clear, candidates for confirmation are asked to renew their baptismal promises as part of the confirmation celebration. The *Constitution on the Liturgy* calls the celebration of the eucharist the source and summit of Christian life. We are baptized for life at the table of the eucharist. The unrepeatable personal transformation effected by confirmation builds on that of baptism, preparing us for this life at the table and in the world. Eucharist is the completion of both baptism and confirmation – it alone is repeatable. When we share in communion with the rest of the Church we renew, deepen and strengthen what God has done for us in baptism and confirmation.

Introduction to Alive in the Spirit!

Role of the Christian community

For Catholics, the parish community carries the responsibility for initiating new members. Each Sunday the parish community gathering for eucharist is a visible sign of the wonders that God has done and is doing in their lives. Confirmation candidates look to the Christian family to be a witness to what they believe. The catechetical method used in this program encourages the candidates to be present and involved with their Sunday community on a regular basis.

The parish community also prepares and supports its adult members who act as leaders and assist in preparing the candidates. You, as such a leader, are a witness and role model for the candidates.

The parish community can expand its involvement in a variety of ways. You might find in the following list of suggestions one or two activities that your parish would like to adopt.

- Invite individual parishioners to pray for a specific candidate throughout the preparation.

- Recruit parish members to prepare and set out the refreshments for the catechetical sessions.

- Invite candidates and their families to a parish potluck at the beginning of the preparation process.

- Include a prayer for the confirmation candidates, their families and the catechists in the general intercessions at Sunday Mass.

Family involvement

Because parents are the primary educators of their children in faith development, *Alive in the Spirit!* encourages you to invite them to join their children in the catechetical sessions. All adults – parents and catechists – would be full participants in the ritual and the catechesis on the experience. By including parents, you will be providing them with a richer understanding of the preparation process.

The candidate's book also encourages families to be actively involved in confirmation preparation. Each session of *Alive in the Spirit!* includes a letter home inviting the family to complete activities with the candidate and offering practical suggestions for fostering a Catholic way of life. The completion of specific pages or activities will enhance the preparation process. (The monitoring of work done at home is not part of the sessions, although the candidates are invited to share their responses.)

Readiness to celebrate the sacrament

Sacraments are celebrations of our relationship with God, celebrated in the midst of the believing community. God continually invites us into relationship, and our response to this invitation is evident in the way we live our lives. A hallmark of a Catholic lifestyle is gathering for Sunday eucharist and striving to live a Christian lifestyle. ("The Eucharist is the source and summit of the Christian life." – *Catechism of the Catholic Church*, 1324) For those capable of it, the acquiring of knowledge or mastery of a list of topics provides necessary nourishment and further stimulation of the ongoing and fundamental response to God's call.

Liturgy and catechesis

When liturgy and catechesis are woven together we are led deeper into the mystery of living as disciples – what we pray informs how we live.

This close relationship between liturgy and catechesis is fostered in *Alive in the Spirit!* The primary importance of gathering for eucharist is highlighted. In part, confirmation is understood as leading us deeper into life in Christ and into full participation in the eucharist.

Immediate preparation for confirmation is an opportunity for catechesis, not religious education. *Alive in the Spirit!* assumes that candidates have been involved in ongoing religious education. Although catechesis and religious education often intersect and mesh, they are different.

- *Religious education* follows a set curriculum of doctrinal knowledge and is intended to provide ongoing education for the learner in an age-appropriate manner. It is an important part of the ongoing non-sacramental program or course of study offered in school or by the parish.

- *Catechesis* provides mentoring for the ongoing conversion of the heart and the way of life. It relies on the awakening and deepening of faith, particularly in light of the experience of life within the Christian community, its liturgical life and its apostolic work in the world.

The catechesis in this program is meant not simply to prepare the candidates to celebrate the rite of confirmation, but to prepare them to live as full members of the Christian community and to participate actively in both the life and mission of the Church. The catechetical method relies on the Church's ancient practice for the formation of newly baptized Christians.

Because the catechesis is experiential, it begins with a ritual. The catechesis following the ritual is mystagogical, beginning with the insights of the participants and then shaping those insights by drawing on the tradition of our Church.

Meeting the needs of all children

Because it is experiential, the catechetical method in this program fosters participation by all candidates regardless of their skills or needs. This approach allows everyone to engage at their own level of experience. If there is a participant with specific needs, it is important for you to be in regular contact with the family to ensure that the candidate is engaged in the process.

Organization

Time line

To allow you plenty of time to invite families to consider enrolling in the preparation process, to hold an introductory session with adult family members, and to complete the five preparatory sessions, we recommend that you allow four to six months for the program.

In large parishes it may be necessary to hold the introductory session two or three times over the course of one or two weeks, so that families can adjust their work schedules and other commitments if they need to.

Candidate sessions can be held weekly or bi-weekly, depending on the circumstances of your parish.

Number of candidates

The sessions work bests with 10 to 15 candidates. With advance planning it will be possible to prepare enough catechists to lead several groups, if needed.

The adult leaders

Familiarity with the two roles of the adult leaders (ritual leader and leader of reflection/catechesis) is integral to the preparation process. The adult leaders are encouraged to gather as a group to prepare and celebrate one or more of the rituals. For new ritual leaders, the time spent preparing with other leaders will be invaluable.

Introductory session

The purpose of this first gathering is to:
- welcome the adult members of the families
- share the vision of the resource with them
- offer practical support.

This gathering generally last about 75 to 90 minutes, including time for prayer.

In this introductory meeting, be sure to communicate the following:
- Confirmation is the second sacrament of initiation.
- Eucharist is the third and only repeatable sacrament of initiation. It nourishes lifelong growth in Christ.
- The celebration of eucharist is the source and summit of our Christian life.
- After confirmation, the candidates will be fully initiated and will continue to gather each Sunday with the Christian family.
- Preparing to celebrate a sacrament is a time of catechesis, not religious education.

- The approach of *Alive in the Spirit!* is experiential, which means that the active participation of candidates is key.
- The whole family is involved in this time of preparation. The parents and sponsors are invited to participate fully in the sessions. All people who gather for the sessions will be praying together and reflecting together. The candidate's book will help to encourage participation at home and in the larger community. Each family is encouraged to choose activities that suit them.
- The expectations and role of a sponsor.

On a practical level, let everyone know:
- That they will need to provide a copy of the child's baptismal certificate (if their child was baptized in another parish, they will need to get verification from that parish, which takes time).
- Details about the time and location of the five preparatory sessions and the sixth session following confirmation.
- Information about a retreat and rehearsal (if you are planning them).
- Information about the date and time of the celebration of confirmation.
- Information about particular parish customs (such as the renting of gowns, etc.).

Turn to the Reproducible Pages section at the back of this book and make enough copies so you can distribute to each family a copy of:

- Word List
- Questions Families Often Ask
- How Is Confirmation Celebrated? (It may be more appropriate to wait until the end of Session 4 or 5 to distribute How Is Confirmation Celebrated?)

Explain that the Word List contains words used during the preparation sessions that may be unfamiliar to the candidates. Families can use the list to help candidates learn them.

Sessions

There are six sessions, each lasting about 90 minutes, including time for gathering and for simple refreshments. Five sessions are held before confirmation and the final session is held the week after confirmation has been celebrated.

Two leaders are required for each session and an ideal group size would be 10 to 15 candidates. To encourage full participation it is best for the candidates to remain in the same group for all five preparatory sessions and for the same catechists to lead them. If leading the preparation is to be shared by more than one team, it is important that all leaders be fully aware of the focus of all the sessions.

The five preparatory sessions follow the same pattern.

Gathering

This is the time for welcoming everyone, making announcements, and sharing an initial conversation about the focus of the session.

Ritual experience

This time of prayer includes a ritual designed to provide an experience somewhat similar to one of the actions of the baptismal rite.

Getting in touch with the experience

Immediately after the ritual experience the participants are invited to reflect on their experience. This part is simply a recall of the ritual without any catechesis or conversation.

Catechesis on the experience

The catechesis proceeds in three phases:

1. from sensory experience to hints about God
2. from God communicating by means of the ritual action to reasons for the use of that action in baptism
3. from the intent of baptism to my life in the Christian community.

Connecting with confirmation and eucharist

The catechesis flowing from the experience will be linked to preparing for living as confirmed members of Christ's body.

Bringing the session home

Before ending the session, the leader will remind the participants of how their families can be further involved before the next session, and also make any announcements.

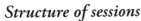

Refreshment Break

Special features

The Leader's Guide provides:
* a helpful note to the catechist
* essential steps in preparing yourself
* information on the goals for each session
* a list of needed supplies
* notes on how to prepare the gathering and ritual areas
* in Session 3, an adaptation for the visually impaired.

The environment

Each session needs two physical locations:
* *a gathering space* where the candidates will be greeted and an initial conversation or activity will happen. This may also be the space that is used for refreshments.

* a *ritual area* where the ritual can take place. A meeting room close to the gathering area is ideal. It is important that the ritual area have space for flexible seating and furniture that can be moved.

Seldom does a parish have space set aside just for catechetical gatherings, so it is important to be creative and flexible when determining the best place to gather for sessions. Try to find a place that has some privacy and that will have few distractions or interruptions. If you need to use a large place or two different sections of a very large hall, mark off with room dividers or carpeting an area more suited to the size of your group.

Frequently asked questions

Who may be confirmed?

Any baptized person who has not yet been confirmed may celebrate this sacrament. According to Canon 889, if candidates for confirmation have the use of reason they must be prepared to celebrate confirmation, be properly disposed, and be able to renew their baptismal promises.

The local parish is responsible for inviting those who have reached the appropriate age to prepare for and celebrate confirmation. Candidates do not have to request in writing to receive this sacrament. They are preparing to complete the initiation that was begun in baptism, not seeking membership in a local group or club.

It is also important to remember that candidates do not need to demonstrate a certain level of knowledge. In particular, candidates with special needs or limited cognitive abilities are to have access to the sacraments. Their parents can determine the best time to answer the Church's call to bring their child to the sacrament. Because *Alive in the Spirit!* is experientially based, candidates with special needs will find sacramental preparation easy.

Do the candidates participate in a retreat before confirmation?

This is a local parish decision. *Alive in the Spirit!* includes an outline for a retreat. See page 97. If you decide to hold a retreat, the best time is after Session 5 when all the other preparations have been completed.

Are candidates for confirmation required to celebrate the sacrament of reconciliation?

Candidates for confirmation have the same responsibilities as all Catholics. As explained in Canon 988, they are bound to confess grave sins, and are also encouraged to confess venial sins. If a candidate for confirmation has never celebrated the sacrament of reconciliation, an invitation to prepare for and celebrate the sacrament is extended, but the Church may not and does not keep a record of those who celebrate the sacrament of reconciliation.

What are the requirements for a sponsor?

Each candidate for confirmation is to be accompanied by a sponsor. If possible, the godparent from baptism is encouraged to serve as sponsor. The sponsor should be a Catholic who is at least sixteen years old, has already been confirmed, has received the eucharist, and is living a life of faith. The sponsor is meant to be a role model and mentor for the candidate. A parent may not serve as a sponsor. (See Canons 892, 893, 874§3.)

Do candidates choose a confirmation name?

Candidates are always confirmed with their baptismal name. It is not necessary for them to choose an additional name.

When is confirmation celebrated?

This depends on local parish practices. Confirmation may be celebrated during one of the regularly scheduled Sunday liturgies, or, in some circumstances, at a time separate from Sunday liturgy. Although it is always preferable to celebrate the sacraments within Mass, confirmation may also be celebrated outside Mass. Even when eucharist is not included, the celebration always begins with the liturgy of the word. See page 106 for further details.

Do confirmation candidates serve as liturgical ministers?

During the celebration of confirmation it is most appropriate for members of the parish to perform the liturgical ministries of hospitality, lector and cantor. Some candidates may be asked to bring the gifts of bread and wine to the altar.

Is there special clothing for confirmation candidates?

Since an alb is the garment of the baptized, it has become customary in some parishes for candidates to wear white gowns. This is not necessary; candidates may simply wear their "Sunday best."

In the past candidates have sometimes been asked to make a stole. Because a stole is a symbol of ordination, it is a garment worn by a deacon, priest or bishop. It is inappropriate for confirmation candidates to wear stoles.

Where should candidates and sponsors sit?

It is best for candidates and sponsors to sit together near the front of the church. This also eliminates the need for elaborate seating plans.

Local circumstances (including the number of candidates and the size of the church) will determine whether reserved seating is necessary or whether candidates and sponsors may sit with families in the body of the church.

Understanding the Explanatory Rites

We are all familiar with the essential baptism ritual: immersion in water or pouring water on the head, and the words, "I baptize you in the name of the Father, and of the Son, and of the Holy Spirit." In an emergency, says the Church, this is all that is required.

But in the full celebration of the sacrament, other actions follow that proclaim dimensions of the sacrament that are present, but not obvious, in the water bath. (For more about baptism as "bath," see *Catechism of the Catholic Church*, 1216.) These ritual actions, which are as much for the benefit of the rest of the assembly as they are for the person being baptized, drive home the fact that baptism conforms us to Christ, transforming us to be like Christ and to share his life.

Anointing after baptism

The Church uses three sacred oils – the oil of the sick, the oil of catechumens, and chrism – that are consecrated by the diocesan bishop at the Chrism Mass celebrated during Holy Week.

- The anointing of the sick is for comfort, healing and strength in time of suffering.

- The anointing of catechumens is for strengthening throughout the period of the catechumenate.

- Chrism is perfumed and is used in four anointings:
  1. in an explanatory rite in the baptism of someone who will not be confirmed immediately
  2. in the celebration of the sacrament of confirmation
  3. in the celebration of the sacrament of holy orders
  4. in the anointing of the church walls and the altar within the rite of dedication of a church and an altar.

Anointings have been associated with baptism since at least the early third century. Their meaning and form as well as their timing within the initiation rites varied widely from place to place and time to time. The earliest written reference to an anointing *after* baptism is from the early third century.

Today, at the moment of the post-baptismal anointing, the minister says, "God the Father of our Lord Jesus Christ has freed you from sin, given you a new birth by water and the Holy Spirit, and welcomed you into his holy people. He now anoints you with the chrism of salvation. As Christ was anointed Priest, Prophet and King, so may you live always as a member of his body, sharing everlasting life." These words show how the baptismal anointing symbolizes that the newly baptized has become like Christ. This anointing speaks of being part of the work, the mission of Christ.

- *A priest* is a messenger between God and people, carrying a message of God's love to the earth and prayer from the earth back to God.

- *A prophet* is a person who reminds people of God's truth and ways.

- *A king* is a person whose responsibility is to look after those he is in charge of; rules are for the good of the people, not for the king.

Timothy Fitzgerald explains this post-baptismal anointing in these words: "This is clearly a 'Christ' anointing, a 'priest, prophet and king' anointing, a 'living body of Christ' anointing ... the 'becoming like Christ the Anointed One' anointing, where we reveal who this child now is and to whom this newborn now belongs ... we crown the child on the top of the head, on the whole person, to symbolize this one is becoming like Christ. This regal anointing is 'on the crown of the head.' This is now a royal child, a priestly, royal, prophetic child, part of the Anointed One."[1]

Although the anointing following the water bath of baptism and the anointing in the sacrament of confirmation are similar in form, they convey different meanings. After a prayer and the laying on of hands, at the moment of the confirmation anointing the minister says, "N., be sealed with the Gift of the Holy Spirit." This confirmation anointing is also related to identity with Christ, but speaks of the anointing with the Spirit that Christ now shares with the Church. (See *Catechism of the Catholic Church*, 690 and 739.)

Clothing with a white garment

The earliest references to the white garments of the baptized are found in the Book of Revelation (7:14). This suggests that they were used in the celebration of the sacrament at the time the book was written. Or perhaps it simply inspired a later practice.

Early writings indicate that clothing the baptized in a white garment after baptism may have been part of the celebration by the late third century, but was done without much ceremony. In those early years, those being baptized were brought into the baptistery (a separate building at that time), stripped of their clothing, and led naked into the pool-sized baptismal font. There, after denouncing Satan, they professed their faith in the triune God and were dunked under the water three times. When they came out they needed to be re-clothed and brought into the liturgical assembly to join in the celebration of the eucharist. Here they would share the sign of peace, join in intercessory prayer, pray the Lord's prayer, and share in the eucharistic meal – all for the first time. The white garment is not specifically mentioned in the earliest instructions, but as time passed, increasing attention was paid to the act of re-clothing, to the radiance of the candidates, and finally to the white garment.

The colour white still resonates with contemporary popular culture; for most of us, white speaks of newness and purity. Church regulations allow for the use of another colour in cultural traditions where colours have different meanings.

This rite proclaims that baptism makes us more than just followers of Christ: we are members of Christ's body. We

---

1. Timothy Fitzgerald, *Infant Baptism: A Parish Celebration* (Chicago: Liturgy Training Publications, 1994), 54.

have taken on his identity: "In him we live and move and have our being" (Acts 17:28). The minister's words during this ritual action point to the change in the person and acknowledge the role of the Christian community in the believer's life. "N., you have become a new creation, and have clothed yourself in Christ. See in this white garment the outward sign of your Christian dignity. With your family and friends to help you by word and example bring that dignity unstained into the everlasting life of heaven."

When adults or older children are baptized at the Easter Vigil they are sent to change from "old clothes" into the new white baptismal garment. Our Church invites these newly baptized to wear their baptismal garment to Sunday Eucharist throughout the great fifty days of Easter, so that they will not forget their new identity. At a celebration of infant baptism the babies often arrive already clothed in white – usually a long gown, but sometimes a white suit – and are baptized by pouring water on the head. In this situation, the action of clothing with a white garment consists in simply touching the white garment the child is already wearing. (In the unusual situation where the baby does not have a white garment, the minister simply touches the baby with a piece of white cloth.) But increasingly, parishes are following the instructions in the ritual book more closely and are baptizing infants by immersion, a practice that requires that the baby arrive in easily removed baby clothes and be clothed in the baptismal garment only after the water bath and anointing.

Presentation with a lighted candle

The story of Jesus' encounter with the Samaritan woman at the well, his cure of the man born blind, and his raising of Lazarus have been proclaimed during the Lenten preparation for initiation since at least the late third century. The promise of the first and last of these stories is addressed in the core action of baptism, the water bath ritual. Though the earliest evidence of the presentation of a lighted candle as a formal part of the celebration of baptism dates only to the sixteenth century, some early accounts of celebrations in the Eastern Church talk about "the enlightenment of baptism" and enlightenment is a recurring theme in baptismal texts throughout the centuries. Under these circumstances it seems almost inevitable that a ritual centred on Christ the light of the world would become part of the baptismal ritual.

Jesus called himself the light of the world: "I am the light of the world. Whoever follows me will never walk in darkness but will have the light of life" (John 8:12).

But Jesus did not stop at calling *himself* the light of the world. In the Sermon on the Mount, Jesus told his followers that *they*, too, are the light of the world: "You are the light of the world. A city built on a hill cannot be hid. No one after lighting a lamp puts it under the bushel basket, but on the lampstand, and it gives light to all in the house. In the same way, let your light shine before others, so that they may see your good works and give glory to your Father in heaven" (John 5:13-16).

St. Paul writes to the Corinthians, "We walk by faith, not by sight" (2 Corinthians 5:7). In baptism we receive the light of Christ, our faith is awakened, and we have Christ and the Spirit as our guides. The words spoken by the minister during this part of the rite associate faith with light. For infants the minister prays during this rite: "May he (she) keep the flame of faith alive in his (her) heart."

Older children and adults are instructed, "Keep the flame of faith alive in your heart."

Ephphetha

The ephphetha (EFF-uh-thuh) rite has been part of the baptismal process since at least the fourth century. Throughout our history it has taken several forms – a simple touching, or accompanied by anointing, by placing salt on the tongue, or by the act of breathing on the candidate – and has involved various senses: eyes, ears, mouth, nostrils, palms, etc. It was often celebrated in association with a series of exorcisms, but always *before* the water bath ritual.

The *Constitution on the Sacred Liturgy* (1963) called for a rite of baptism specifically for celebration with infants (children too young to benefit from catechesis). At that time the catechumenate was defunct, the same ritual was used for people of all ages, and godparents spoke for infants in the parts where a spoken response was required of the candidate. Although the *Rite of Christian Initiation of Adults* retains the ephphetha as a preparatory rite celebrated with adults and older children on Holy Saturday, just hours before the celebration of the sacraments of initiation, the revision of the rite for infants places the ephphetha rite – for the first time in our history – *after* the water bath among the explanatory rites.

The name of the rite is taken from the word spoken by Jesus in the gospel of Mark when he cured a man who could not hear or speak (Mark 7:34). Mark explains that the word means "Be opened." In this rite, the candidate's ears and mouth are touched and the Church prays that the child may be open to profess the faith they hear to the praise and glory of God. The *Rite of Christian Initiation of Adults* explains that this rite expresses our need for God's grace in order to truly hear the word of God and profess it.

The ephphetha rite draws our attention to the fact that we are totally dependent on God. It uses our ears and mouth to stand for our whole being; the Church prays that the newly baptized will always be open to recognize and acknowledge the presence and the action of God – however they are revealed – with their whole being and throughout their lives.

Session 1

Baptized with Water

Note to the catechist

Preparing for confirmation includes broadening our understanding of the relationship between baptism and the weekly celebration of Sunday eucharist. Baptism and confirmation are sacraments of initiation that prepare and lead the newly baptized, the newly confirmed to full participation in the celebration of eucharist.

The five preparatory sessions explore through ritual, reflection and catechesis the relationship between the sacramental signs of baptism and life as a disciple of Christ. Confirmation, the completion of our baptism, strengthens us to live as full members of the eucharistic community. It supports us as we live as disciples of Jesus and members of God's family.

When the sacrament of baptism is celebrated with immersion the person walks into a pool of water and is plunged under water three times while the Trinitarian formula, "I baptize you in the name of the Father, and of the Son, and of the Holy Spirit," is pronounced. The newly baptized emerges from the water bath soaking wet and aware of water's power to cleanse and its potential to destroy. This experience of baptism is one that not all have shared. For many, water is poured over the head while the Trinitarian formula is pronounced. Baptism into the life, death and resurrection of Jesus is the result of either experience.

Young people may be led to reflect on how they live differently because they have been joined to Jesus in his passage from death to resurrected life. They may also be led to reflect on the support and strength they require and receive from the members of God's family.

Young people are immersed in a culture that is filled with symbols. The task of sorting through the sometimes overbearing images and events is not an easy one. Those who journey with young people need to assist them in making sense of so many different experiences. Your role as catechist is to assist them in using the Church's perspective to interpret rituals and sacramental signs.

In this first session water is used in a ritual action. Celebrating with water and reflecting on the celebration are the essential elements of the session.

Preparing yourself

- Be familiar with the organization of the session and the words you will say.

- Decide who will be the ritual leader and who will lead the reflection.

- Learn the following acclamation: *Blessed be God, O blessed be God.* It is taken from the refrain of the hymn "Who calls You by Name" by David Haas.

Goals

Session 1 is intended to help the candidates:

- become aware that God speaks to us in the actions of sacramental rituals

- gain an understanding of why water is used in the celebration of baptism

- be introduced to confirmation as a sacrament in which God strengthens us for the life to which we are called at baptism: life at the eucharistic table and in the world.

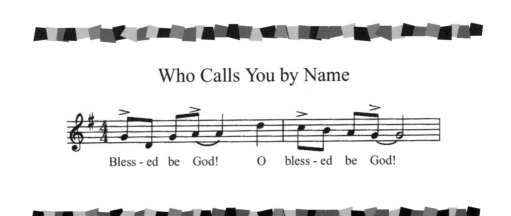

Who Calls You by Name

Bless - ed be God!   O   bless - ed be God!

Supplies and Environment

- a name tag for each person
- a table
- a white tablecloth
- a cross
- a Bible or lectionary
- a copy of the adapted text of John 3:1-16 from page 103
- a large empty bowl or tub
- a jug (or several jugs, if necessary) of water
- a second large empty bowl
- nourishing snacks for the break

Before the session

Prepare two areas as follows:

The Gathering Area

Arrange in a circle or semi-circle comfortable, age-appropriate chairs, mats or cushions for each person. (For suggestions about the gathering and rituals areas see the The environment, on page 15.)

Have on hand:
- a name tag for each person the jug (or several jugs, if necessary) of water
- the cross
- nourishing snacks for the break.

The Ritual Area

Arrange in a circle or semi-circle comfortable, age-appropriate chairs, mats or cushions for each person. Be sure everyone has a clear view of the centre.

Place in the centre a table covered with a white cloth. Be sure that it is large enough to also hold a jug of oil, a baptismal garment and a large candle, which will be added in future sessions.

On the cloth, place
* the Bible or lectionary opened at John 3:1-16, with the duplicated page discreetly inserted
* the large empty bowl or tub.

Leave room on the cloth for the jug(s) of water and the cross.

Gathering

Greet the participants as they arrive and take them to the gathering space. Before you begin the session, attend to any housekeeping matters (the location of washrooms, the importance of name tags, the plan for a break, the importance of participating and not distracting others, etc.).

Distribute the names tags and invite everyone to write their names on them and then to share their first name and tell one thing about their name (e.g., what it means, why they were given it,

who else in their family has the same name, why they like or dislike their name, etc.).

Introduce the session in words such as:

Today water will be an important part of our session. How many different ways have you used water today?

Invite comments.

Conclude with words such as:

We are going to move to another space where we will use water in a special way. You will need to use all your senses: sight, sound, touch, smell, taste, and your memory.

Before moving, teach the acclamation that will be used. The leader sings, "Blessed be God" and all respond, "O blessed be God." If singing is not possible, echo-speak the words energetically.

Form the group into a procession. The adult who is not leading the ritual should lead the procession carrying a cross. The ritual leader should go last, carrying the jug of water. If more than one jug of water is used, recruit candidates to carry the extra ones. These water-carriers should bring the jugs of water to their places and wait for your signal before placing the jugs on the white cloth.

Ritual experience: water bath

1. The group should end the procession from the gathering area to the prepared ritual area around the table (or cloth if you are using the floor).

Place the cross and the jug of water on the cloth and signal for the extra jugs of water, if any, to be put in place.

2. Say:
On the day of your baptism you were claimed for Christ. As you prepare to celebrate the sacrament of confirmation, the Christian community holds you in its heart.

Then approach each person, including the other adult leader, and sign each one on the forehead with the sign of the cross, using the whole hand, saying:

N., the Christian community greets you joyfully again today with the sign of Jesus' cross, by which he has claimed you.

3. When your have signed everyone, invite the participants to sit. Take the Bible from the cloth and read the inserted adapted text from John 3:1-16. Then return the Bible to its place on the cloth.

4. After a few moments of silence, say:

As we prepare to celebrate confirmation we enter again into the celebration of our baptism and explore what God has done for us in water.

Take the jug of water and hold it aloft for all to see, saying:

Blessed are you, Lord our God. Father, Son and Holy Spirit, in water you tell us of the wonders of your power and love.

Sing: **Blessed be God!**
All respond: *O blessed be God!*

Pour about one quarter of the water into the tub or bowl and say:

**Blessed are you, Lord our God.
At the beginning of time, you created the world and separated the land from the waters of the sea and sky and life came forth in goodness and holiness.**

Sing: **Blessed be God!**
All respond: *O blessed be God!*

Pour another quarter of the water into the tub or bowl and say:

Blessed are you, Lord our God. When Moses and his people were living as slaves you led them through the waters of the Red Sea, to freedom in a new

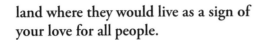

land where they would live as a sign of your love for all people.

Sing: **Blessed be God!**
All respond: *O blessed be God!*

Pour another quarter of the water into the tub or bowl and say:

Blessed are you, Lord our God. When John baptized Jesus in the waters of the Jordan River, you proclaimed that he is your beloved Son.

Sing: **Blessed be God!**
All respond: *O blessed be God!*

Pour the remaining water into the tub or bowl and say:

Blessed are you, Lord our God. After he rose from the dead, Jesus told his followers, "Go out and make disciples of all nations baptizing them in the name of the Father, and of the Son, and of the Holy Spirit."

Sing: **Blessed be God!**
All respond: *O blessed be God!*

5. Set aside the empty jug and, standing beside the tub or bowl, say:

Now, Loving God, by this water may we remember all that you have done for us.

Put your hands as far into the water as possible and show that you enjoy the experience of the water. Smile; take obvious pleasure. Your actions will give the participants permission to have fun and enjoy the water, too. They will follow your example. It is possible to "play" in the water with respect. The intent is to experience the water in a full way.

Suggested actions:
- rubbing water onto your face and arms
- gently splashing water onto your face
- picking up handfuls of water and allowing it to run through your fingers.

Step back and use an open arm gesture to invite the group to come forward. Say:

Come to the water.
Come in silence.
Put your hands into the water as far as you can. Feel the water on your face and arms.
Experience the water in silence.

It is important that everyone participate in this activity far beyond the usual dipping of a finger and sign of the cross. If they are reluctant, invite them individually by gesture or by name.

Alive in the Spirit!
Leader's Guide   **18**

After the participants have gone to the water, they should return to their place and remain standing. When everyone has had a turn, gesture for all to sit.

6. After a few moments of silence, gesture for everyone to stand. Say:

Loving God,
everything we see and hear,
everything we smell, taste and feel,
everything that happens in life,
gives us a hint
of what you are really like.

Help us to understand your love
and guide us to live loving lives,
so that all people may know you
and walk in your ways.

We ask this in the name of Jesus and by the power of the Holy Spirit.

All respond: *Amen.*

Getting in touch with the experience

At this point, the two adult leaders change roles. The ritual leader should not lead the reflection and catechesis.

To call the group back to focus sing or say: **Blessed be God!**
All respond: *O blessed be God!*

Invite the participants to recall the experience of the water ritual in these or similar words:

Think about everything that has happened so far. We experienced God's gift of water in this room.

Use the following questions, one at a time, to help everyone remember the water ritual. Wait for responses. Do not be afraid of silence. Allow everyone a chance to respond before moving on to the next question. Do not to pressure anyone to speak.

Encourage the participants to expand their answers beyond one or two words. If a single-word answer is offered, ask **"What was splashing?"** or **"What did the water do?"** or **"What did it sound like?"** You can ask for a fuller answer by asking: **"Can you tell me more about that?"**

If candidates are reluctant to answer, try one of these ideas.

- Invite one of the more outgoing individuals to begin.
- Name a moment in the ritual, then repeat the question, e.g., **"When N. poured the water, what did you hear?"**
- Ask the candidates to recall how the ritual began, then repeat the question.

What did you hear?

Hoped-for responses
water splashing; people laughing; giggling; water pouring; words said; people moving; the leader speaking; interesting words; names; specific events; different forms of water

What did you hear N. say?

Hoped-for responses
names (Moses, John the Baptist, Jesus); specific interesting words; specific events

What did you see?

Hoped-for responses
lots of water; clean, clear water; some water fell on the floor; water falling; water pouring; a beautiful jug; a big, beautiful bowl (or tub); people using the water; the specific action of a certain individual; everyone enjoyed the water

What did you feel?

Hoped-for responses:
cold or warm water; water on my face and hands; wet face, arms, hands; my skin feels fresh; my clothes got a little wet; nervous, excited, shy, happy

What did you do?

Hoped-for responses
I touched the water; I got water on my sleeve; I watched people

Is there anything else you remember?

Hoped-for responses
Answers will vary.

Thank the participants for their answers.

Break

Announce the break, and then offer the participants a nourishing snack. Because of food allergies, keep the snack as simple and natural as possible (fresh fruit pieces, etc.).

Catechesis on the experience

The session now moves from a reflection on the sensory nature of the experience to the catechesis based on the experience.

Phase 1
from sensory experience to hints about God

Phase 2
from God communicating by means of water to reasons for the use of water in baptism

Phase 3
from the intent of baptism to my life in the Christian community

The questions and sample comments are offered as suggestions to encourage dialogue. Use their responses to deepen the reflection and the catechesis.

Phase 1

Initial Reflection on the Experience

In this first phase, you will rely mainly on the insights of the participants.

Assemble the group in the ritual area. Call the group back to focus, by singing or saying: **Blessed be God!**
All respond: *O blessed be God!*

Invite everyone to sit silently and recall the ritual actions. Invite them to look once again at the water. Highlight or recap the words offered by the group before the break. Then say:

Water was a part of our ritual. We could have chosen something other than water, like sand or salt. But we didn't. For just a moment think of what water says to you about God.

Allow for a moment or two of reflection and invite responses.

Hoped-for responses

- God is refreshing like water.
- God quenches my thirst like water.
- Water gives life – so does God.
- Water makes plants grow – God helps me to grow.
- There was lots of water – God is big, too.

Offer encouragement by repeating or rephrasing some responses. At the beginning, an adult may need to offer a response to help the candidates. It is not necessary to have a specific number of responses.

Phase 2

Connecting with Baptism

In this phase, you will be doing more and more of the talking, introducing new and important ideas.

Remind everyone of their own baptism using these or similar words:

When you were younger your family asked for you to be baptized. You and your family came to the church. Probably there were other families there with children to be baptized. There were also people from your parish present – a priest or deacon. If you were baptized during Sunday liturgy, there were probably many people.

Continue by explaining that during baptism they were immersed in water or maybe water was poured over their head. Invite the participants to imagine how this may have felt. Then say:

At the time of your baptism the Church, the Christian community, chose water. Why do you think the Church uses water at baptism?

Remind the participants that earlier we talked about how water refreshes, helps plants grow, and gives us life – we cannot live without water. After a moment of silence, invite responses.

Hoped-for responses

- The Church wants us to know that baptism, like water, gives us life.
- Water is necessary for life and baptism is necessary for life in Christ.
- Too much water kills plants or people; in baptism we are not destroyed but sin is.

Ensure that the following points are covered:

- Water is used as a sign of the life that God has given to us.
- Water is used as a sign of our new life in Christ.

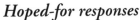

Phase 3

My Life in the Christian Community

At this point present the following catechesis on baptism and the call to a Christian lifestyle.

Baptism changes us forever. It draws us into God's life in a new way. All baptized people share this amazing life in God. St. Paul wrote that baptism takes away all distinctions between believers. He said: *"In Christ Jesus you are all children of God through faith. There is no longer Jew or Greek, there is no longer slave or free, there is no longer male or female; for all of you are one in Christ Jesus." (Galatians 3:26-28)*

This means that in the eyes of God we are all equal members of God's family. Each of us is called to live a Christian lifestyle that reflects our unity and equality.

Connecting with confirmation and eucharist

Continue with the catechesis by asking: **How do our families or the parish community help us to live as members of God's family?**

Allow for comments. Make sure the following points are included:

- Our families help us by praying with us, teaching us how to care for others as Jesus does, going to church together.
- The parish helps us by gathering every Sunday so that we can learn how to live as members of God's family.
- The parish leaders teach by example and often by being involved at our school or at religious education programs at the parish.
- The parish community helps by preparing us for confirmation, a sacrament that helps us live as members of God's family.

Say:

Our Church's liturgy helps us to remember that our new life in baptism lasts forever. During our liturgy we are reminded that our baptism has changed us forever.

Discuss together the various times that water is used to remind us of our baptism. Here are some examples you can use.

- the baptismal font at the entrance of the church or holy water holders at the doors of the church

- the sprinkling rite during the Easter Vigil and throughout the Easter season (Note that during the Easter Vigil or on Easter Sunday we renew our baptismal promises. This is our opportunity to recall the promises that were made in baptism. At the beginning of the confirmation rite we also renew our baptismal promises.)

- the sprinkling of the casket with holy water at a funeral.

Bringing the session home

Ask candidates to open their books to page 5. Remind them that there is a letter for their families on page 6, some pages to read together (pages 7 and 8), and three pages, "My Baptism Story" on page 9 and "Renewing Our Promises" on pages 10 and 11, to read and complete before the next session

Conclusion

Announce the date and time of the next session. Make sure the candidates write the date and time in the space provided in the family letter on page 6. Then ask the candidates to turn to the prayers on pages 12 and 13 in their books. Invite them to pray these prayers each day with a member of their family. Then say the prayer on page 13 together.

Before ending the session, remind everyone to take their personal belongings with them and to make sure that both the ritual space and the gathering space are tidy.

Alive in the Spirit! Leader's Guide **34**

Session 2

Anointed with Oil

Note to the catechist

Session 2 continues to explore the relationship between the sacramental signs of baptism and life as a disciple of Christ by considering the anointing with sacred chrism (KRIZ-um). This anointing, during the rite of baptism for infants and others who will not be confirmed immediately, follows the pouring of water and the Trinitarian formula. Anointing with chrism is the first of four "explanatory rites." These rites lead us to a deeper or broader understanding of the meaning of baptism.

Chrism is also used in confirmation. But the uses of chrism in baptism and confirmation have different meanings. At the moment of the post-baptismal anointing, the minister says:

God the Father of our Lord Jesus Christ has freed you from sin, given you a new birth by water and the Holy Spirit, and welcomed you into his holy people. He now anoints you with the chrism of salvation. As Christ was anointed Priest, Prophet and King, so may you live always as a member of his body, sharing everlasting life.

These words show how the baptismal anointing symbolizes that the newly baptized has become like Christ.

The confirmation anointing is also related to identity with Christ, but speaks of the anointing with the Spirit that Christ now shares with the Church. After a prayer and laying on of hands, at the moment of the confirmation anointing the minister says:

N., be sealed with the Gift of the Holy Spirit.

In this session oil is used in a ritual action. Celebrating with oil and reflecting on the celebration are the essential elements of the session.

Background

The Church uses three sacred oils: the oil of the sick, the oil of catechumens, and chrism.

- The anointing of the sick is for comfort, strength and healing in times of sickness. Often a person suffering from a serious illness or facing major surgery asks to celebrate the anointing of the sick.

- The anointing of catechumens is for strengthening the catechumen (unbaptized) on his or her journey. Babies may be anointed with the oil of catechumens before baptism. This is known as a preparatory rite.

- The third sacred oil is chrism. Chrism is perfumed oil used in four anointings:

1. in an explanatory rite in the baptism of someone who will not be confirmed immediately
2. in the sacrament of confirmation
3. in the sacrament of holy orders
4. at the anointing of the church walls and the altar within the rite of dedication of a church and an altar.

Preparing yourself

- Be familiar with the organization of the session and the words you will say.

- Decide who will lead the ritual and who will lead the reflection.

- Review the acclamation: *Blessed be God, O blessed be God.*

Goals

Session 2 is intended to help the candidates:

- understand why oil is used in the celebration of baptism
- understand that baptism calls us to a special way of life
- continue to learn how in confirmation God strengthens us for the life to which we are called at baptism: life at the eucharistic table and in the world.

Supplies and Environment

- a name tag for each person
- a chair, mat or cushion for each person
- a small stand to hold the book for the ritual (a black music stand is an ideal size)
- a table
- a white tablecloth
- a cross
- a Bible or lectionary
- a jug of water
- a jug of perfumed olive oil (not real chrism); it is important to use a sufficient amount of scent so that the perfume is apparent (available in some specialty stores)
- a second large empty bowl
- paper or cloth towels
- snacks

Before the session

Prepare two areas as follows:

The Gathering Area
Arrange the seating as in Session 1. Have on hand:
- a name tag for each person
- the jug of perfumed oil
- the cross
- nourishing snacks for the break.

The Ritual Area
Arrange the seating as in Session 1, and put the table and cloth in the centre of the space.

On the cloth, place:
- the Bible opened at Luke 4:16-21
- the large bowl of water
- the second large empty bowl.

Leave room on the cloth for the cross and jug of oil. Place the small stand near to where the leader will stand during the ritual action. In a convenient place nearby, have an ample supply of cloth or paper towels.

Gathering

Greet everyone as they arrive and take them to the gathering space. Before beginning, attend to any housekeeping details (location of washrooms, the importance of participating and not distracting others, the plan for a break, etc.). Distribute the name tags.

Review together page 9 in their books and invite the candidates to share something they discovered about their baptism or the baptism of a family member. For example: the date, name of the church, their age at the time of baptism, the date of a family member's baptism, godparents' names, etc. It is not necessary for each candidate to share, but allow sufficient time for those who wish to share to do so.

Thank them for sharing and review the refrain used in Session 1, "Blessed be God, O blessed be God." Ask one of the candidates to carry the ritual book during the procession and place it on the stand in the ritual area.

Introduce the session in words such as:

Today oil will be an important part of our session. In what ways do you use oil at home?

Invite comments. Encourage the participants to name various types and uses of oil. If necessary, you can remind them that there are many different types of oil: cooking oil, massage oil, baby oil, oil for cars, WD40 (an oil for tight or stiff locks), oil for burning in lamps.

Conclude with words such as:

We are going to move to another space where we will use oil in a special way. We will pray and sing the response we used at our last session. You will need to use all your senses: sight, sound, touch, smell, taste, and memory.

Form the group into a procession. The adult who is not leading the ritual should lead the procession, carrying a cross. The ritual leader should go last, carrying the jug of oil.

Ritual experience: anointing

1. The group should end their procession around the table. Place the cross and jug of oil on the cloth.

When everything is ready, say:

On the day of your baptism you were claimed for Christ. As you prepare to celebrate the sacrament of confirmation, the Christian community holds you in its heart. Remember that God loves you.

2. Then go to each one present, including the other leader, and sign each person on the forehead with the sign of the cross, using the whole hand, saying:

N., the Christian community greets you joyfully again today with the sign of Jesus' cross, by which he has claimed you.

3. When your have signed everyone, invite them to sit. Take the Bible from the cloth and read Luke 4:16-21. Then return the Bible to its place on the cloth.

4. After a few moments of silence say:

As we prepare to celebrate confirmation we enter again into what happened at the celebration of our baptism. In the story I just read, Jesus announced that the Spirit of the Lord has anointed him. When we were still wet with baptismal water we were anointed with sacred perfumed oil, chrism, on the crown of our head.

Take the jug of perfumed oil, hold it aloft for all to see and say:

Blessed are you, Lord our God, Father, Son, and Holy Spirit, in oil you tell us of the wonders of your power and love.

Lower the jug of oil and sing:
Blessed be God!
All respond: *O blessed be God!*

Raise the jug of oil again and say:
Blessed are you, Lord our God. At the beginning of time you commanded

trees to grow, giving us their fruit. From the olive tree, we take oil that enriches our lives in many ways.

Lower the jug of oil and sing:
Blessed be God!
All respond: *O blessed be God!*

Raise the jug of oil again and say:

Blessed are you, Lord our God. Long ago you commanded Moses to consecrate Aaron his brother as a priest, by the pouring of oil, setting him aside as a messenger with a message of love from God and a prayer from the people of earth.

Lower the jug of oil and sing:
Blessed be God!
All respond: *O blessed be God!*

Raise the jug of oil again and say:
Blessed are you, Lord our God. Over and over you anointed prophets like Amos, Isaiah and Micah to go among your people with words of warning when they strayed from your ways and words of comfort when they longed to see your face.

Lower the jug of oil and sing:
Blessed be God!
All respond: *O blessed be God!*

Raise the jug of oil again and say:
Blessed are you, Lord our God. You

sent Nathan with a jug of oil to call David from his flock and anoint him as king to shepherd your people.

Lower the jug of oil and sing:
Blessed be God!
All respond: *O blessed be God!*

5. Stand beside the table near the large empty bowl. Hold the jug of oil and say:

Now, Loving God,
by this oil may we remember who you have called us to be.

Step back and use an open arm gesture to invite the group to come forward. Say:

Come to the oil.
Come in silence.
Open your hands.
Feel the oil on your hands.
Enjoy the oil in silence.

Invite the other adult leader to come first to the table with palms up over the empty bowl. Pour a small amount of oil, about the size of a quarter, in one palm of the adult, who rubs her or his hands together so that the oil will be absorbed.

Invite the participants one by one to

approach the table and do the same.

After receiving the oil they should remain standing at their places. After all have come to the table, gesture for everyone to sit.

6. After a suitable period of silence, gesture for everyone to stand. Say:

Loving God,
everything we see and hear,
everything we smell, taste and feel,
everything that happens in life,
gives us a hint
of what you are really like.

Help us to understand your love and guide us to live loving lives, so that all people may know you and walk in your ways.

We ask this in the name of Christ your Son and in the power of the Holy Spirit.

All respond: *Amen.*

(If needed, give everyone paper towels to wipe the oil from their hands. In order to maintain the session's momentum, it is important not to send people to wash their hands.)

Getting in touch with the experience

At this point, the two adult leaders change roles. The ritual leader should not lead the reflection and catechesis.

To call the group back to focus, sing or say: **Blessed be God!**
All respond: *O blessed be God!*

If necessary, repeat two or three times.

Invite everyone to recall the experience of the oil ritual in these or similar words:

Think about our conversation earlier about oil at home.
Think about how we experienced God's gift of oil.
Think about the scripture, the prayer and our actions.

Use the following questions to help participants recall the oil ritual. After each question is asked allow time for silence and responses. Each person need not speak. It is important to relax, allow for silence, and encourage everyone to respond, but without forcing anyone to speak. Encourage the participants to go beyond a one-word answer.

If they are hesitant, you may begin by asking one of the more outgoing participants or you could say something like, **When N. was holding the jug of oil, did you hear any special names?**

What did you hear?

Hoped-for responses
a story about Jesus in the temple; people laughing; giggling; reacting to the oil; singing; people moving; words about God; the leader speaking; interesting words: crown of my head, king, shepherd, warning, comfort, prophet, priest, messenger (message), olive (tree), chrism; specific names (Isaiah, Micah, Amos, Aaron, David); specific events

What did you see?

Hoped-for responses
shiny, golden oil; lots of oil; oil in a large jar; oil being poured; my skin became shiny; the oil went into my skin; people moving

What did you feel?

Hoped-for responses
oil on my hands; smoother skin; warmth from rubbing my hands together; nervous, excited, shy, happy; my skin feels slippery

What did you smell?

Hoped-for responses:
a beautiful smell; the oil smelled nice; oil mixing with my cologne or perfume.

Is there anything else you remember?

Hoped-for responses
Answers will vary.

Conclude by acknowledging how well everyone remembered. Then announce the break.

Break

Offer everyone
a nourishing snack.

Catechesis on the experience

The session now moves from a reflection on the sensory nature of the experience to the catechesis based on the experience.

Phase 1
from sensory experience to hints about God

Phase 2
from God communicating by means of oil to reasons for the use of oil in baptism

Phase 3
from the intent of baptism to my life in the Christian community

The questions and sample comments are offered as suggestions to encourage dialogue. Build on the words of the participants and use their responses to deepen the reflection and the catechesis.

Phase 1

Initial Reflection on the Experience

In this first phase, you will rely mainly on the insights of the participants.

Assemble the group in the ritual area.

Call the group back to focus by singing or saying: **Blessed be God!**
All respond: *O blessed be God!*

Invite everyone to sit silently and recall the ritual actions. Invite them to look once again at the oil and at their hands. Recap the words offered by the group before the break. Say:

Oil was part of our conversation at the beginning and it was an important part of our ritual. We know that everything comes from God. For just a moment think of what oil says to you about God.

After a moment or two of reflection, invite responses.

Hoped-for responses
- The oil smelled nice; maybe God wants us to smell good things.
- My skin was shiny and soft; God is soft to touch. God touches me softly.
- My skin was sparkling with oil; God believes I am special and can sparkle just like my skin.
- The oil seemed to disappear yet it was still present. Maybe God is like this.

Say: **Think of the ways we use oil at home. What might that say about God?**

Hoped-for responses

- Baby oil protects the baby; God protects us.
- Oil makes things operate better; God makes our lives better, smoother.
- Oil helps heal our bodies; God can heal us.

Encourage the participants by repeating or rephrasing some responses. At the beginning, one of the adults may need to offer a response to help the candidates begin. It is not necessary to have a specific number of responses.

Thank everyone for their responses.

Phase 2

Connecting with Baptism

In this phase, you will be doing more and more of the talking, introducing new and important ideas.

After the phase one responses, remind the participants that both water and oil were used at their baptism. Say:

The oil that is used during baptism is blessed oil, called sacred chrism (KRIZ-um). Chrism is a special perfumed oil that is blessed by the bishop each year before Easter. Today we used oil with perfume, not sacred chrism.

Describe how the priest anointed their head with sacred chrism. The anointing is on the crown of the head. The oil is poured and the priest traces the cross on the crown of their head. Explain that at baptism the Church, the Christian community, chose both water and oil – although it sounds silly or strange, we could have used sand and salt, or maybe juice and cream. Ask:

Why do you think the Christian community uses perfumed oil at baptism?

Encourage them to explore the idea that perfumed oil is used because it tells us we are special and that the smell or scent of the oil is a sign that something is different.

Discuss the action of anointing. Highlight the difference between anointing a person and using oil on our own skin. Point out that someone else anoints us for a specific reason.

Invite the participants to think of people or times we anoint someone or something in our world. Some of them may recall the anointing at the beginning of the movie "The Lion King."

Listen to their responses. You may prompt them by reminding them of some of the things said about oil at the beginning. If necessary, remind them that oil is used to protect our bodies,

to protect food from burning, to make something work better, to preserve wood. Conclude this section by explaining that just as our family uses different oils for different reasons so, too, our Church uses different oil for different reasons.

Briefly explain the three oils used by our Church:

The Church uses three sacred oils: the oil of the sick, the oil of catechumens, and chrism. The anointing of the sick is for comfort, strength and healing in times of sickness. Often a person suffering from a serious illness or facing major surgery asks to celebrate anointing of the sick. The anointing of catechumens is for strengthening the catechumen (unbaptized) on his or her journey. Babies may be anointed with the oil of catechumens before baptism. This is known as a preparatory rite. The third sacred oil is chrism.

Ask: **Why do you think the Christian community anoints us with sacred chrism at our baptism?**

Listen to their responses. Highlight the following points:
- We are anointed to remind us that we are part of God's royal family.
- The chrism reminds us that we have been joined to Jesus and given a special task or job.

- The sacred chrism reminds us that new life in Christ touches all parts of us.
- Christ dwells within us.

Share the words said prior to the anointing with chrism:

God the Father of our Lord Jesus Christ has freed you from sin, given you a new birth by water and the Holy Spirit, and welcomed you into his holy people.
He now anoints you with the chrism of salvation. As Christ was anointed Priest, Prophet and King, so may you live always as a member of his body, sharing everlasting life.

Move to the next phase by inviting the participants to think of how we are called to live differently because of our baptism.

Phase 3

My Life in the Christian Community

Present the following catechesis on baptism and living a Christian life.

Remind everyone that through baptism we have been changed forever; we have become part of God's holy people, a royal family. The baptized have a very special job to fulfill. We are to live as disciples and continue the work of Jesus in the world. Our baptism is a beginning, not an ending. As disciples we are called to live a certain way. Jesus is our role model for living as disciples. Ask:

What did Jesus do? How did he live?

Hoped-for responses
Jesus cared for others: he helped them, taught them about God, loved those who were mean to him, forgave people when they hurt others, told stories about God, lived the message that he taught.

Ask: **How can we as disciples live like Jesus?**

Listen to the responses. Encourage them to be specific in their comments. For example we can live as disciples by caring for the poor in our community, by praying for those we love and those who hurt us, by standing up for what is right in our school yards and at home.

Conclude this phase by acknowledging that it is not always easy to live as a disciple. Sometimes it becomes difficult because our friends or peers may tease us or we may feel uncomfortable. But God's Spirit will help us know the right way to act.

Connecting with confirmation and eucharist

Ask: **Who helps us to live as disciples?**

Allow for comments, then remind the participants that our families help us by praying with us, going to church together, and caring for others the way Jesus did. Our parish helps us by praying with us on Sunday and leading by example. In our parish some of the ways we live as disciples are: being part of the youth group, assisting with special projects like Out of the Cold, being part of the St. Vincent de Paul Society, helping with events like parish picnics, participating in outreach programs, serving as liturgical ministers, visiting the sick or shut-ins, etc.

Explain that Jesus has sent the Holy Spirit to guide us so that we may live as his disciples. Recall that earlier we heard a reading from the gospel where Jesus described himself as being anointed and sent to do good works. Note that at baptism we are anointed and reminded that we are part of God's royal family forever. As part of this family we are anointed as priest, prophet and king.

Explain briefly:

- A priest is a messenger between God and people, carrying a message of God's love to the earth and prayer from the earth back to God.

- A prophet is a person who reminds people of God's truth and ways.

- A true king is a person whose job is to look after those he is in charge of; rules are for the good of the people, not for the king.

Grasping the full meaning of being anointed priest, prophet and king may be challenging, so assure the candidates that Jesus does not expect us to live this way without assistance.

In confirmation we are anointed with sacred chrism and we are sealed with the gift of the Holy Spirit. Explain that the gift of the Holy Spirit cannot be described easily. We use seven words or traits to describe this gift. Three of them are *understanding, wisdom* and *courage*.

It may be possible to help the candidates to grasp the role of the gifts of the Holy Spirit by discussing how we are led to make decisions or choices when we take time to stop and reflect before acting.

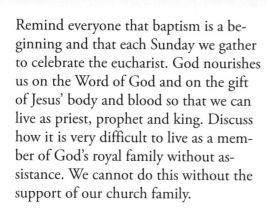

Remind everyone that baptism is a beginning and that each Sunday we gather to celebrate the eucharist. God nourishes us on the Word of God and on the gift of Jesus' body and blood so that we can live as priest, prophet and king. Discuss how it is very difficult to live as a member of God's royal family without assistance. We cannot do this without the support of our church family.

Assure them that we will learn more about living as disciples during the upcoming sessions.

Bringing the session home

Ask candidates to open their books to Session 2 on page 14. Remind them that there is a letter for their families on page 15. Encourage them to read "Oil in Church," "My Life in the Christian Community" and "Co-operating with God's Spirit," on pages 16, 17 and 18. Remind them that they should read "Your Sponsor" on page 19, and read and complete "Working for the Kingdom of God" on page 20.

Conclusion

Announce the date and time of the next session. The candidates should write the date and time in the space provided in the family letter on page 15. Ask the participants to wear a special piece of clothing to the next session. The clothing could be special because it is a favourite colour, a gift, is worn to all sporting events, feels comfortable, was worn to a family event such as a wedding or celebration, etc.

Ask the candidates to turn to the prayers on pages 21 and 22. Invite them to pray these prayers each day with a member of their family. Together say the prayer on page 22.

Before ending the session, remind the participants to take their personal belongings with them and to make sure that both the ritual space and the gathering space are tidy.

Clothed in Christ

Note to the catechist

This session explores "Clothing with Christ," the second of four explanatory rites that follow the water bath in baptism. Although the full effect of baptism is accomplished in the water ritual, the explanatory rites point to a deeper meaning or dimension of the sacrament that may not be easily apparent.

The practice of dressing the newly baptized in a white garment dates from at least the mid-fourth century and the Book of Revelation in the New Testament also uses this symbolism. Even in twenty-first-century North American culture, the colour white still speaks of newness and purity. And in our culture, various articles of clothing, like a prom dress or a sports-team shirt, can hold special significance.

The act of clothing the newly baptized in a special garment is at the core of the rite; the colour white is important, though secondary. For this reason the catechesis in this session, although it addresses the Church's use of the colour white, pays more attention to the action of donning the garment than to its specific colour.

Today a baby usually arrives at the church already dressed in a white gown or white suit and baptism is accomplished by pouring water. When this happens, the clothing with a white garment consists of the minister touching the baby's white gown. However, more parishes are implementing the ancient practice of baptizing by immersion. When this happens, the baby is dressed in the white garment after the water bath. When adults or children of catechetical age are baptized at the Easter Vigil they are sent to change from "old clothes" into new white baptismal garments. Our Church invites the newly baptized to wear their baptismal garment to Sunday Eucharist throughout the great fifty days of Easter.

Being clothed in a baptismal garment is a visible sign of an invisible change brought about by the water bath. The rite of the Church points to the change in the person and acknowledges the role of the Christian community in the life of the believer.

The Church proclaims:

N., you have become a new creation, and have clothed yourself in Christ. See in this white garment the outward sign of your Christian dignity. With your family and friends to help you by word and example, bring that dignity unstained into the everlasting life of heaven.

Note that the garment is not simply a uniform or baptism gift or souvenir. The minister's words clearly explain its meaning. This act of donning new clothing reveals the taking on of a new identity. Baptism makes us more than just followers of Christ; we are members of Christ's body. We have taken on his identity: "In him we live and move and have our being" (Acts 17:28). Putting on a baptismal garment is putting on Christ; we are part of Christ now. The candidates may find this truth challenging or difficult to grasp. The mystery of being joined to Christ can never be fully defined or explained.

The Cross

During baptism the child is signed with the cross during the preparatory rite. The sign of the cross is used in this session to further open up the character of Christian life. The new life and new identity we are given in baptism come through Christ as a result of his death and resurrection. The empty cross and sign of the cross speak of both his death and resurrection. Christ is our invisible garment forever, but we cannot wear our white baptismal garment forever. Using the cross helps us to remember that we have put on Christ.

World Youth Day Cross

At the conclusion of the Holy Year of Redemption (1983–1984), Pope John Paul II gave the youth of the world a large wooden cross and asked them to carry it to the world as a sign of Jesus' love for all humanity. He told them, *"My dear young people, at the conclusion of the Holy Year, I entrust to you the sign of this Jubilee Year: the Cross of Christ! Carry it throughout the world as a symbol of Christ's love for humanity, and announce to everyone that only in the death and resurrection of Christ can we find salvation and redemption."* This cross is known as the World Youth Day Cross. The World Youth Day Cross travelled across Canada in preparation for World Youth Day in Toronto in 2002.

Preparing yourself

- The ritual is shorter than the first two sessions and the reflection and catechesis are longer.
- Be familiar with the organization and words you will say.
- Wear or bring a special piece of clothing to this session.
- Decide who will lead the ritual and who will lead the reflection.
- Review the acclamation:
  Blessed be God! O blessed be God!

Goals

Session 3 is intended to help the candidates:

- understand why we are clothed in a special white garment during the celebration of baptism
- expand their appreciation for meaning and importance of the cross
- understand that in confirmation God strengthens us for the life to which we are called at baptism: by our own lives to show Christ to those around us and to the whole world.

Supplies and Environment

- a name tag for each person
- a small stand to hold the book for the ritual (a black music stand is an ideal size)
- a chair for each person
- special clothing worn or brought by the leaders
- an alb
- a table
- a white tablecloth
- a cross
- a Bible or lectionary
- a copy of the adapted scripture text based on a combination of Galatians 3:27, 28b and Philippians 2:5 from page 103
- a large bowl of water
- a jug of perfumed oil (not real chrism)
- snacks

Alive in the Spirit!
Leader's Guide **50**

Before the session

Prepare two areas as follows:

The Gathering Area
Arrange the seating as in previous sessions. Have on hand:
- a name tag for each person
- the cross
- nourishing snacks for the break.

The Ritual Area
Arrange the seating as in previous sessions, and put the table and cloth in the centre of the space.

On the cloth, place
- the Bible or lectionary with the duplicated page inserted discreetly
- the large bowl of water
- the jug of perfumed oil (not real chrism)
- the alb (if it will not fit on the table, put a chair behind the table and drape the alb over it)

Leave room on the cloth for the cross.

Place the music stand close to the spot where the leader will stand during the ritual action.

Gathering

Greet the participants as they arrive and take them to the gathering space. Before you begin the session attend to any housekeeping details.

Distribute name tags and if necessary review the importance of participating and not distracting others.

Invite the candidates to share some of the responses they wrote in their books after Session 2. You may need to review together page 20, before asking candidates to share some of their responses. Affirm their answers and encourage anyone who did not record activities to mark down one or two ideas that apply to their family. It is not necessary for each person to share information, but allow sufficient time for those who wish to share to do so.

Thank them for sharing, and then review the refrain "Blessed be God, O blessed be God."

Introduce the session in words such as:

On the day of your baptism the Church gave you baptismal clothing. Today we will look at the importance of baptismal clothing and what it represents. We asked you to wear a special piece of clothing to our session. It may be special for many reasons: a gift, a favourite colour, a lucky sweater.

Invite the participants to share something about the special piece of clothing they have worn to the session. It is important that the leaders participate and share something about the special clothing they have worn, too. Give enough time for everyone to speak. It is not necessary for each person to share information.

Thank them for their participation and conclude with words such as:

We are going to move to another space where we will recall being clothed in a special way. We will pray and sing (or say) the response we used at our last session. You will need to use your senses of sight, sound, touch, and memory.

Review the acclamation "Blessed be God, O blessed be God" and then form the group into a procession. The adult leader who is not leading the ritual should lead the procession carrying a cross. The ritual leader should go last, carrying the ritual book.

Ritual experience: clothed in Christ

1. After the group has processed from the gathering area to the prepared ritual area, they should finish their procession around the table. Place the cross on the cloth. When everyone has arrived and settled, sing or say the response "Blessed be God, O blessed be God" and then say:

On the day of your baptism you were claimed for Christ.
As you prepare to celebrate the sacrament of confirmation, the Christian community greets you joyfully and holds you in its heart.
Remember that God loves you.

Because you will be using the sign of the cross as part of the ritual experience, omit the usual sign of the cross greeting now.

2. Invite the participants to sit. Take the Bible from the cloth and read the adapted text. Then return the Bible to its place on the cloth.

3. After a few moments of silence say:

As we prepare to celebrate confirmation we enter again into what happened at the celebration of our baptism. In the passage I just read, St. Paul is speaking to the Christians of Galatia. He is telling them that those who have been baptized have been clothed in Christ. He also tells them that baptism has changed them. At the time of our baptism, after we were anointed on the crown of our head with chrism, St. Paul's words were spoken to us and we received baptismal clothing.

4. Go to the participant beside you and invite that person to stand. Trace a large cross on the front of the participant without touching. The cross you make should stretch from head to toe and from one side of the body to the other.

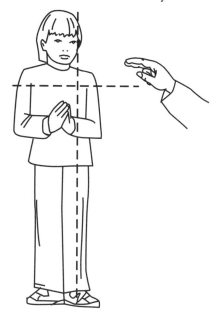

As you are tracing the cross, say:

N., you have become a new creation, and have clothed yourself in Christ.

With a gesture, signal this person to remain standing.

Sing: **Blessed be God!**
All respond: *O blessed be God!*

5. Repeat all of step 4 with everyone. Be sure to include the other leader.

Adapting the Ritual
To make it possible for sight-impaired participants to experience this part of the ritual, you can use an open hand to trace a cross on the forehead, feet and shoulders.

6. When everyone has been signed with the cross, invite all to stand in silent prayer for a moment.

7. After a suitable period of silence say:

**Blessed are you, Lord our God
for new living things:
for baby brothers and sisters
for all living creatures
or seeds and plants.**

Sing: **Blessed be God!**
All respond: *O blessed be God!*

Say:
**Blessed are you, Lord our God
for new beginnings:
for the first day of holidays,
for birthdays, for the morning.**

Sing: **Blessed be God!**
All respond: *O blessed be God!*

Say:
**Blessed are you, Lord our God for our new life:
for Jesus,
for the family of God,
for new ways of being in the world.**

Sing: **Blessed be God!**
All respond: *O blessed be God!*

Say:
Loving God,
may we remember all that you have
done for us. Guide us to reflect Christ
to others, so that all people may know
you and walk in your ways.

**We ask this in the name of Christ
your Son and in the power of the Holy
Spirit.**

All respond: ***Amen.***

Getting in touch with the experience

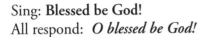

At this point, the two adult leaders
change roles. The ritual leader should
not lead the reflection and catechesis.

To call the group back to focus sing or
say: **Blessed be God!**
All respond: *O blessed be God!*

If necessary repeat two or three times.
Invite everyone to recall the experience
in words such as:

**Think about our conversation earlier
about special clothing.**
**Think about the scripture reading and
our actions.**

Use the questions that follow to help
recall the ritual. Allow for silence after
the questions and between responses.
Encourage everyone to respond, but it
is not necessary for everyone to speak.
Encourage the participants to go beyond
one-word answers.

What did you hear?

Hoped-for responses
*a story about becoming a new creation,
singing, words about being clothed in
Christ, my name, the words "Blessed be
God."*

What did you see?

Hoped-for responses
*a cross being traced on people, people
standing, people smiling, people singing*

How did you feel?

Hoped-for responses
a little embarrassed, nervous, happy

Is there anything else you remember?

Hoped-for responses
Answers will vary.

Conclude by thanking them for their participation. Then announce the break.

Break

Offer everyone a nourishing snack.

Catechesis on the experience

The session now moves from a reflection on the sensory nature of the experience to the catechesis based on the experience. It will unfold a little differently from the sessions on the water bath and the anointing. Phases 1 and 2 rely on what the participants heard – the scripture text, the ritual text; Phase 3 relies on the experience of the cross.

Phase 1

from sensory experience to hints about God through exploring the metaphor of Christ as an item of clothing

Phase 2

from God communicating by means of created things to reasons for the use of special new clothing at baptism, including the relationship between the baptismal garment and the cross

Phase 3

from the intent of baptism to my life in the Christian community

Phase 1

Initial Reflection on the Experience

Assemble the group in the ritual area. To call the group back to focus, sing or say:
Blessed be God!
All respond: *O blessed be God!*

Remind the participants that on the day of baptism the newly baptized is clothed with a white garment. Explain that before we speak about the white garment we will use our imaginations. Invite the participants to think for a moment or two in silence about:

* what type of clothing they would want to be
* if they could wish for just one piece of clothing, what they would choose.

You may want to give a few examples: a blanket, a basketball jersey, a ski suit, etc. Invite comments from the group.

Continue by reminding everyone that the Church announces, *"You have become a new creation and clothed yourself in Christ."*

Then ask:

If Christ were a piece of clothing that you could put on, what might it look and feel like?

Allow time for silent reflection before inviting responses.

Hoped-for responses

The responses will vary. Ask people to explain their responses and follow up their responses so that small details are identified. For example, if the response "a large robe" is offered, ask about its colour and texture.

Thank everyone for their responses and remind them that there are no "correct" or "incorrect" answers.

Phase 2

Connecting with Baptism

In this phase, you will be doing more of the talking, introducing new and important ideas. Remind everyone that at their baptism the Church explained that baptism has given them a new identity. Remind them that when we join a team or when we go to a particular school we are often given new clothing, a uniform. The uniform identifies us as belonging to a particular group.

Explain that the Church chooses a big white alb as our baptismal garment. Describe how the alb is large enough to cover our entire body.

Ask: **Why is the alb white?**

Hoped-for responses
> White is a colour of life, purity, newness.

Ask:

Why do you think the Church chooses a large piece of clothing?

Hoped-for responses
> Christ touches every part of who we are; it is large enough for all people; baptism is for everyone so a large garment fits all people just like baptism is for all people.

Ask:

Why does the Church choose have us wear a new piece of clothing at baptism?

Hoped-for responses
> to remind us that we are a new creation; to tell us that we have joined a special group; to help us visualize putting on Christ.

Thank them for their responses. Highlight that in baptism we have become a new creation and have put on Christ. Our new identity means that we have put on Christ.

Then ask:

What is the most important thing Jesus did?

Allow time for reflection and then invite responses. The answers will vary. When someone shares that dying on the cross is the most important thing Jesus did, explain that the cross is the sign of our new identity. The cross is our constant reminder that we have put on Christ and have put on the mind of Christ. Tell the participants about the World Youth Day Cross that Pope John Paul II gave to the youth of the world. (See p.49.) The cross is our visible sign of what it means to live as a disciple of Christ, to be clothed in Christ.

Recall that during our ritual the cross was traced over our entire body. This reminded us that no part of us has been left untouched by baptism. Our Christian identity touches every part of who we are. A cross was traced on our entire body to remind us that our identity as Christians is linked to Jesus' death and resurrection.

Discuss how for some people a cross is worn as a piece of jewellery or an accessory, but for others a simple wooden, silver, or gold cross is a sign of something much more. For followers of Christ a cross worn around the neck can be a visible reminder that we have Christ as our identity. It is Christ that we are joined to. The cross is a reminder of Jesus' death and resurrection and of what has happened to us in baptism.

Demonstrate making the sign of the cross on yourself and then ask:

When are some of the times we trace a cross on ourselves?

Hoped-for responses
- at the beginning and end of prayers
- as we enter a church
- at the beginning of Mass
- at the time of the gospel
- when we leave church
- when we pass a church
- when we drive past a cemetery

Invite everyone to think for a few minutes about how we are meant to live differently because we are identified with Christ.

Phase 3

My Life in the Christian Community

Remind everyone that Jesus' death on the cross and his resurrection are linked to the cross. The cross is a symbol of self-giving so that others may live fully. The mystery is that when we give of ourselves not only do others live fuller lives but so do we.

Because our baptism identifies us with Christ and his cross, we are called to live differently. We are to be visible signs of Christ working in the world.

Ask:

Can you think of ways you can be a visible sign of Christ in the world?

Allow time for comments. Help them to be specific in their answers. Invite them to name a difficult part about being a Christian. Share one or two examples first. For example, an adult may share that it is sometimes difficult to walk away from co-workers when they are gossiping about another person, or that it can be difficult to ask someone not to tell a racist joke.

Remind the participants that we are called to be Christ, to wear this identity with others. This is not a solitary act. We have help from our families and the Christian community.

Connecting with confirmation and eucharist

In confirmation the Church prays with us that we will be aware of Christ's presence in our lives and that we will discover how to rely on the Spirit to guide us. Recall that Jesus was filled with the Spirit. In baptism we received the Holy

Spirit and in confirmation the Church prays with us that we will know and be aware of the presence of the Holy Spirit in our lives. Explain that it is the strength of the Holy Spirit that helps us to be more like Christ.

Recall that the Church uses seven gifts to describe the Holy Spirit. In previous sessions we have spoken of the gifts of *understanding, wisdom* and *courage*. Two other gifts are *right judgment* and *reverence*. Explain that it can be challenging to learn how to listen to the Holy Spirit. We need to spend time listening. As disciples we listen by praying both alone and with others.

Continue by explaining that Jesus taught people in many ways. Often he would teach people by sharing a meal with them. Explain that Jesus still teaches at a meal. Each Sunday when we gather for eucharist we are taught through the Word of God being proclaimed, and we are fed by God with the gift of Jesus' body and blood. It is important for the entire community to gather for this special meal.

Bringing the session home

Ask the candidates to open their books to Session 3 on page 23. Remind them about the letter for their families on page 24. Explain that they are to read and complete "The Cross" on page 25, "My Life in the Christian Community" on page 26, and "Gifts of the Holy Spirit" on page 27 before the next session. Encourage them to read "Christian Symbols" and "The Communion of Saints" on pages 28 and 29.

Conclusion

Announce the date and time of the next session and have the candidates write this information in the space provided in the family letter.

Ask the participants to bring their baptismal candle to the next session. Explain that if the candle has been burnt or misplaced they may bring a simple 10-inch taper.

Ask the candidates to turn to the prayers on pages 30 and 31. Invite them to pray these prayers each day with a family member. They could take turns leading the prayer. Then together recite the prayer on page 31.

Before ending the session, remind everyone to take their personal belongings with them and to make sure that both the ritual space and the gathering space are tidy.

Enlightened by Christ

Note to the catechist

This session explores the presentation of the lighted candle, the third of the four explanatory baptismal rites. The parents, godparents and the entire assembly are reminded that this child has been enlightened by Christ. The parents and godparents are also reminded that they are to keep the candle burning brightly:

Receive the light of Christ.
Parents and godparents
this light is entrusted to you to be kept burning brightly.
These children of yours have been enlightened by Christ.
They are to walk always as children of the light.
May they keep the flame of faith alive in their hearts.
When the Lord comes,
May they go out to meet him
with all the saints in the heavenly kingdom.

Jesus called himself the Light of the World: "I am the light of the world. Whoever follows me will never walk in darkness but will have the light of life" (John 8:12). All light and life finds its source in God. The light of Christ always reveals God. Those enlightened by Christ recognize the presence of God and are led by the Spirit in the ways of God.

But Jesus did not stop at calling himself the Light of the World. He told his followers that they, too, are the light of the world: "You are the light of the world. A city built on a hill cannot be hidden. No one after lighting a lamp puts it under the bushel basket, but on the lampstand, and it gives light to all in the house. In the same way, let your light shine before others, so that they may see your good works and give glory to your Father in heaven." (Matthew 5:14-16)

The participants will begin this session by remembering many different sources of light and exploring the need for light in our lives. We know that light from the sun makes it possible for plants and animals to thrive. The energy that we rely on to play, sleep and work comes from the food we eat, which has received its energy from the sun. The energy from the sun is stored inside us and keeps us healthy. We can feel the energy and effects of the sun and how it makes a difference in our lives.

Some Practical Considerations

Since Session 4 requires the parish paschal candle, determine ahead of time whether the candle and its stand can be moved to your ritual area. If they cannot be moved, find out whether the group can meet where the paschal candle is. If you cannot use the paschal candle, use a large pillar-style candle.

If you are using the paschal candle, determine whether it can be easily removed from its stand for use in the procession from the gathering area to the ritual area. If not, simply place the paschal candle in the ritual area ahead of time and omit it from the procession. (You can use a lantern in the procession.)

This session requires the participants to use lit candles. Although safety suggestions are included, you and the rest of the catechetical team can decide whether any additional measures are needed for your group. Note the location of the fire extinguisher and telephone nearest the gathering and ritual areas. If you have a cell-phone make sure it will work in the space you will be using. Plan ahead and use reasonable caution.

If you have serious concerns about using lit candles, you can prepare a deep tub of sand or salt into which the candles can be placed.

Preparing yourself

- Be familiar with the organization and words you will say.

- Decide who will lead the ritual and who will lead the reflection.

- Review the acclamation:
  Blessed be God, O blessed be God.

Goals

Session 4 is intended to help the candidates:
- understand why a candle is used in the celebration of baptism
- expand their appreciation of the meaning and importance of sharing the light of Christ
- understand the role of confirmation in their lives.

If you cannot use the parish paschal candle, use a sizable pillar-style candle instead. You can decorate this candle (using non-flammable materials). If you do not use the paschal candle in the procession, use a lantern.

Supplies and Environment

- the parish paschal candle and its stand
- matches or a lighter
- the baptismal candle of each participant (or 10-inch tapers for those who do not bring their baptismal candle)
- a baptismal candle (your own or one of the kind given by the parish)
- a candle snuffer
- a name tag for each person
- a chair, mat or cushion for each person present
- a table
- a white table cloth
- a cross
- a Bible or lectionary bookmarked at John 8:12 and Matthew 5:14-16
- a jug or bowl of water
- a jug of perfumed oil (not real chrism)
- an alb
- a small stand, such as a music stand, to hold the book during the ritual
- nourishing snacks for the break

Before the session

Prepare two areas as follows:

The Gathering Area
Arrange the seating as in previous sessions.

Have on hand:
* a name tag for each person
* the parish paschal candle (or another large candle)
* matches or a lighter
* the candle snuffer
* the cross
* nourishing snacks for the break.

The Ritual Area
Arrange the seating as in previous sessions, and put the table and cloth in the centre of the space. If the paschal candle cannot be moved from its place in the church, set up the table and its contents somewhere near the paschal candle.

On the cloth, place:

* the Bible or lectionary opened at John 8:12
* the jug or bowl of water
* the jug of oil
* the alb

Place the paschal stand and the candles for the participants nearby, as well as a small stand to hold the book during the ritual.

If you are not using the paschal candle and stand, prepare a sturdy table to use as a stand for your pillar-style candle. The table should have a large surface to make it less likely for the candle to be knocked over.

Leave room on the cloth for the cross.

If you have concerns about using lit candles, you could place the candles in a deep tub of sand or salt at the centre of the ritual area. Around the edge of the tub distribute place markers with the candidates' names on them.

Lower the level of lighting for the space. If the overhead lighting cannot be dimmed sufficiently, turn off the overhead lighting and place a small lamp at the periphery of the space to provide dim lighting. Ensure you have quick access to a fire extinguisher and telephone in case of accident.

Gathering

Greet the participants as they arrive and take them to the gathering space. Before you begin the session, distribute name tags and attend to any housekeeping matters.

Collect the baptismal candles and ensure that they are labelled or tagged for easy identification. Place the baptismal candles in the ritual area.

Give participants a chance to share their responses from page 25, "The Cross," and page 27, "The Gifts of the Holy Spirit." If necessary provide the candidates with an opportunity to record answers in their books.

Introduce the session in words such as:

Today light will be an important part of our session. Think for a moment before we make a list of different kinds of light.

Allow a moment of silence and then invite the participants to name different kinds of light. If necessary you can provide some prompting: overhead lights, headlights, candles, flashlights, sun, stars, streetlights, computer screens, fire, night lights, matches, glow sticks, dash lights in the car, lighthouses, etc.

Invite participants to explain briefly their favourite kind of light. Extend the conversation by asking questions such as:

- **How does light help us?**
- **Is there any kind of light you do not like?**
- **Does light ever harm us?**

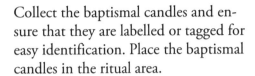

Adapting the Ritual

To make it possible for sight-impaired candidates to participate, make sure the discussion includes some of the non-visual properties of light: most light sources radiate heat as well; plants need light to live.

If the participants have not included the sun as a source of light, mention how important this source of light is and then discuss how light from the sun makes it possible for plants and animals to thrive. The energy that we rely on to play, sleep and work comes from the food we eat, which has received its energy from the sun. The energy from the sun is stored inside us and keeps us healthy. We can feel the energy and effects of the sun and how it makes a difference in our lives.

Conclude this discussion in words such as:

We are going to move to another space where we will pray and sing and use a special candle. You will need to use all of your senses, so it is important not to distract others.

Light the candle (or lantern, if you cannot use a candle).

Say:

Each year at Easter our parish lights a new Easter candle with a holy flame. Now, as we light our Easter candle again (or "Now as we light this candle" or "Now, as we light our lantern") may God make our flame holy as well and chase away the darkness from our minds and hearts.

Form the group into a procession. The adult who is not leading the ritual may invite one of the candidates to carry the cross, lead the procession, and place the cross on the cloth when everyone is in place. The ritual leader should go last, carrying the candle (or lantern).

Ritual experience: enlightenment

1. The group should end the procession from the gathering area to the prepared ritual area around the table (or cloth if you are using the floor).

2. Place the cross on the cloth and the paschal candle in its stand. If the paschal candle was not used in the procession, light it now with a taper from the lantern and then extinguish the lantern.

3. When everything is ready, say:
On the day of your baptism you were claimed for Christ.

As you prepare to celebrate the sacrament of confirmation, the Christian community holds you in its heart. Remember that God loves you.

Then go to each one present, including the other adult leader, and sign each one on the forehead with the sign of the cross, using your whole hand, saying:

N., the Christian community greets you joyfully again today with the sign of Jesus' cross, by which he has claimed you.

4. When you have signed everyone, invite everyone to sit. Take the Bible from the cloth and read John 8:12. Then return the Bible to its place on the cloth.

5. After a few minutes of silence, say:

**As we prepare to celebrate confirmation we enter again into the celebration of our baptism.
On the day of our baptism, after we received our special baptismal clothing, we were given a lit candle.
The flame of the candle came from the Easter candle.**

6. Go and stand next to the paschal candle. Place your hand on the candle and say:

**Blessed are you, Lord our God.
Your glory fills the whole universe.**

Wherever you are, there is brilliant light that cannot be dimmed.

Sing: **Blessed be God!**
All respond: *O blessed be God!*

Place your hand on the candle again and say:

**Blessed are you, Lord our God.
At the very beginning of all things, you made light and separated the light from darkness.**

Sing: **Blessed be God!**
All respond: *O blessed be God!*

**Blessed are you, Lord our God.
You have given us the sun,
a great glowing ball of fire,
to light up our days and energize our whole world.**

Sing: **Blessed be God!**
All respond: *O blessed be God!*

Blessed are you, Lord our God. Even at night when the darkness covers the earth the stars, the planets and the moon blaze in the sky, guiding the lost and reminding us that you never forget us.

Sing: **Blessed be God!**
All respond: *O blessed be God!*

7. Touching the candle, say:

Now, Loving God, with the light of this candle may we remember all that you have done for us.

8. With your hand trace the cross on the candle, saying:

**Jesus Christ is the light of the world.
Christ yesterday, today, forever.
To him and to his Father be glory!**

9. Invite the participants to come forward one by one to the paschal candle. Take each person's baptismal candle (or a taper), light it from the paschal candle, and give it to the person, saying:

N., you have been enlightened by Christ. Walk always as a child of the light.

The participants return to their places and sit holding the lit candle.

If you have decided to use a deep tub of sand or salt to hold the candles, the adult who is not leading the ritual should help the candidates insert their candles into the sand next to their place markers.

After everyone has received a lit taper, take the Bible from the cloth and proclaim Matthew 5:14-16. Then return the Bible to its place on the cloth.

10. After a suitable period of silence gesture for everyone to stand. Say:

Blessed are you, Lord our God. You gave us the gift of your Son. Guide us as we continue to walk in your light. May we reflect your light to others so they will come to know of your love for them. We ask this in the name of Christ your Son and by the power of the Holy Spirit.

All respond: **Amen.**

Getting in touch with the experience

Turn up the lighting to normal levels and show how to extinguish the candles safely. Keep the main candle lit. Tell them to put their candles in a safe place until it is time to leave (they may become a distraction).

At this point the two adult leaders change roles. The ritual leader should not lead the reflection and catechesis.

If necessary, call the group back to focus by singing or saying (two or three times): **Blessed be God!**

All respond: *O blessed be God!*

Invite the participants to recall the experience in words such as:

**Think about our conversation earlier about light.
Recall our procession, the candle and the way the space looked.
Think about the Scripture readings and about all of the lit candles.**

Use the questions that follow to help recall the ritual. Relax and allow for silence. Encourage everyone to respond, but it is not necessary for everyone to speak. Encourage the candidates to go beyond one-word answers.

What did you hear?

Hoped-for responses
a prayer about God and light, Jesus is the light of the world, I am the light of the world, the words "Blessed be God," the words "you have been enlightened by Christ," people singing

What did you feel?

Hoped-for responses
A little nervous because it was darker, unsure about what would happen, the warmth of the candle, wax dripping, the smooth candle

What did you see?

Hoped-for responses
not too much at first because it was darker, a large candle, small candles, shadows from the candlelight, people holding candles, the room getting brighter, a cross being traced on people, people standing, people smiling, people singing.

Is there anything else you remember?

Hoped-for responses:
Answers will vary.

Conclude by thanking everyone for their participation. Then announce the break.

Break
Offer everyone a nourishing snack.

Catechesis on the experience

The session now moves from a reflection on the sensory nature of the experience to the catechesis based on the experience.

Phase 1
from sensory experience to hints about God

Phase 2
from God communicating by means of light to reasons for using lighted candles in baptism

Phase 3
from the intent of baptism to my life in the Christian community.

The questions and sample comments are offered as suggestions to encourage dialogue. Use the words of the participants and their responses to deepen the reflection and the catechesis.

Phase 1

Initial Reflection on the Experience

Assemble the group in the ritual area. To call the group back to focus, sing or say:
Blessed be God!

All respond: *O blessed be God!*

Invite the participants to sit silently and recall the ritual actions. Invite them to look at the lit paschal candle and to recall what they heard, saw and felt. Highlight their comments from before the break.

Say:
At the beginning of our session we talked about many different types of light. During our ritual we lit one large candle, and from it candles for each person. We thanked God for the gift of light in our lives. For just a moment think of what a lit candle says to you about God.

Allow for a moment or two of silence and then invite responses.

Hoped-for responses
- A candle removes darkness and God removes darkness.
- A candle gives warmth and God makes us feel warm.
- The large candle lit all the little candles, so God can give light to all people.
- The burning wax smelt nice; maybe God wants us to smell things that are nice.
- The flame is hot and powerful and God is powerful, too.
- The flame could melt or burn things and God can melt things like sadness or fear.

Thank them for their responses.

Phase 2

Connecting with Baptism

Remind the participants that a lighted candle was presented to them at their baptism. (Refer to the baptismal candles that were brought to the session.) Then ask: **During the celebration of baptism the Easter (paschal) candle is lit. Why do you think the Church does this?**

Hoped-for responses
- The candle reminds us that Jesus is the light of the world.
- The candle is used to light other candles.
- We light candles before we pray or at special times.

Then ask:
Why do you think the Church uses the Easter (paschal) candle at baptism?

Hoped-for Responses
- The Easter candle reminds us of Easter when Jesus rose from the dead.
- Just like Jesus died, we die to sin in baptism.
- Jesus rose from the dead and because we are baptized, we will rise too.
- The candle reminds us that we are joined to Jesus and, like him, we are a light for the world.

Thank the participants for their responses and say: **During the celebration of baptism the newly baptized are given a candle lit from the Easter candle. After the candle is presented the priest says:**

Receive the light of Christ.
Parents and godparents, this light is entrusted to you to be kept burning brightly.
These children of yours have been enlightened by Christ.
They are to walk always as children of the light.
May they keep the flame of faith alive in their hearts.
When the Lord comes, may they go out to meet him with all the saints in the heavenly kingdom.

Ask:
Why does the Church give the newly baptized a lighted candle?

Listen to their responses, and make sure they understand that the candle is a visible reminder that we have been changed through baptism. Remind the participants that after the water bath we are anointed with oil and become part of God's royal family. We also are clothed in Christ – we get a new identity – and then the presentation of the lighted candle tells us that we are to walk as children of the light.

The Church announces that we have been enlightened by Christ. Discuss what it means to be enlightened. Help them to recognize that through baptism we have received the light of Christ and we are able to rely on Christ to show us or help us to know how to live in union with God.

Ask:
What does it mean to walk as children of the light?

Listen to their responses and encourage them to be specific when they describe what it means to walk as children of the light. (For example: Being kind to others is not as specific as choosing to talk to the classmate who is ignored by others. Helping others is not as specific as sharing some of my allowance with the St. Vincent de Paul Society. Volunteering to help others is not as specific as agreeing to help with child care at a parish meeting.) Thank the participants for their sharing.

Phase 3

My Life in the Christian Community

Remind the participants that during our ritual we heard two passages from scripture. Then read John 8:12 again and ask:
What does Jesus say he is?

Allow for responses. Then read Matthew 5:14-16 and ask:

What does Jesus say you are?

Allow for responses.

Then ask:

What does it mean to be light for the world?

Allow for responses (these may be similar to what it means to walk as children of the light).

Ask:

What happens when we are light for the world? (You may need to read Matthew 5:16 again.)

Listen to their responses and tell them that when we let our light shine, others recognize the goodness and they come to know more about God.

Conclude this session by asking how we are able to be light for the world. It may be helpful to remind the participants of the earlier discussion about the sun being an important source of light. Listen to their responses and conclude by presenting the following catechesis on baptism and living a Christian life.

In our sessions together we have reflected on what happened to us at baptism. We know we have become part of God's royal family, have a new identity, and have received the light of Christ. The light of Christ shines through our good works so that the world can be a better, brighter place.

All the baptized are called to be a light for the world. So remember that we are not alone; we have our family, the people at church, and the whole Christian community to help us to grow and walk as children of light.

Connecting with confirmation and eucharist

Remind the candidates that our families and the parish support us as we strive to be a light for the world. The celebration of confirmation is one way we are strengthened to walk as children of the light. During the celebration of confirmation we pray for the Spirit to help us be a light for the world.

Remind the candidates that the Church uses seven gifts to speak about the Holy Spirit. In previous sessions we have spoken of the gifts of *understanding, wisdom, courage, right judgment* and *reverence.* A sixth gift of the Holy Spirit is *knowledge.* The gifts of the Holy Spirit help us to live as children of the light and to be a light for the world.

The gifts of understanding, wisdom and knowledge help us see God and know the ways of God in our heart. Knowing something in our heart is deeper or different than knowing it in our mind. We know in our hearts that God will be with us and that God's Spirit will guide us to walk as children of the light and to keep the flame of faith alive in our hearts.

Continue the catechesis by asking if the participants have ever been camping in a place that is very dark or if they can remember a time when the electricity was off and they needed to rely on candles or flashlights. Share a story of how difficult it is to see in the dark when we have only one candle or one flashlight for many people. Explain that letting our flame of faith shine for others can be difficult if we are doing it alone. Jesus knew that we would need to be with others. Jesus calls us to live and to share our faith in community. This is just one more reason why we gather for eucharist on Sunday. Being with others helps us to keep our flame of faith alive in our hearts so that we can let the light of Christ shine brightly for others.

Bringing the session home

Ask the candidates to open their books to Session 4 on page 32. Remind them about the letter for their families on page 33. Encourage them to read "The Easter Candle" on page 34, and ask them to read and complete "The Light of Christ" on page 35 and "Sharing the Light" on page 36 before the next session.

Conclusion

Announce the date and time of the next session and have the candidates write this information in the space provided in the family letter.

Ask the candidates to turn to the prayers on pages 37 and 38, and invite them to pray these prayers each day with someone in their family. Then together say the prayer on page 38.

Before ending the session, remind everyone to take their personal belongings with them and to make sure that both the ritual space and the gathering space are tidy.

Session 5

Awakened to Grace

Note to the catechist

This session explores the Ephphetha rite (EFF-uh-thuh), which follows the presentation of the lighted candle. *Ephphetha* means "Be opened." This word appears in Mark's gospel when Jesus cures a man who can neither hear nor speak (Mark 7:34). The *Rite of Christian Initiation of Adults* explains that the ephphetha rite or the rite of opening of the ears and mouth symbolizes the need for God's grace in our lives. It is God's grace that enables us to hear and profess the word of God.

The ephphetha rite draws our attention to our total dependence on God. We rely on God's grace for our lives and for our ability to know God. We do not need to do something to gain favour with God and then receive God's grace. Rather, all of creation has come into existence because of the grace of God. God's grace permeates the entire world. The whole world speaks of God. Just as works of art reveal something of the human artists who create them, every thing of nature and every human experience reveals God.

Although we are completely dependent upon God, we are able to ignore God if we choose. God has given us a free will and the ability to know and to love God. During our lives we may choose to embrace – or ignore – the signs of God's presence. Through the gesture of touching our ears during the ephphetha rite the Church prays that we will be able to "hear" God and be open to praising God. The Holy Spirit's gift of wonder and awe in God's presence fosters openness to God and the desire to praise God.

The touching of our lips draws to our attention our need to offer glory and praise to God. A Christian's primary prayer is one of praise and thanksgiving. When we gather for Sunday liturgy we bring our lives and offer to God our prayer of praise and thanks. The eucharistic prayer of the Mass is the Church's great prayer of thanks and praise for all God's gifts to humanity, the greatest of which is Jesus Christ.

Our dependence upon God for all things is foundational. Through the abundant nature of God we are given the gift of life. Through the presence of God in our lives – grace – we are able to offer God our praise and thanks for our life and all its gifts. This relationship is at the very core of who we are. As we come to know God we seek to praise God through our actions and words. We do this not because we are concerned with breaking rules or laws but because our knowledge and awareness of God compel us to live in harmony with our Creator.

This session begins by focusing on receiving messages. We need to be aware of God's presence in our lives before we offer praise to God. We have the freedom to receive messages sent to us or to ignore both the message and the sender. For example, we may choose not to answer a telephone call, not to open a letter, to delete a message from our inbox, or simply to ignore the messenger.

To help the candidates become aware of how God communicates with us, begin the session by focusing on the various ways we receive messages. They also may come to realize that it is sometimes easy to ignore God's messages. We rely on our families and the Christian community to assist us in hearing and responding to God's messages.

As we become open to God we begin to see the world, other people and our lives through the eyes of God. This is referred to as "seeing with the eyes of faith." This vision of the world leads us to give praise and thanks to God.

During this session the participants will not carry anything new in the procession. They themselves are the symbol. It is their ears and lips, their lives that offer praise to God. You do not need to point this out. It will be highlighted during the time of catechesis.

Preparing yourself

- Be familiar with the organization of the sessions and the words you will say.

- Decide who will lead the ritual and who will lead the reflection.

- Review the acclamation:
  Blessed be God, O blessed be God!

Goals

Session 5 is intended to help the candidates:

- understand why the Church prayed at their baptisms that their ears and mouths be opened
- understand that all creation is graced by the presence of God
- review the journey they have taken together and forge its links to the parish Sunday eucharist.

Supplies and Environment

- a name tag for each person
- a chair, mat or cushion for each person
- a table
- a white tablecloth
- a cross
- a Bible or lectionary
- copies of the adapted texts of Matthew 10:16-42 and Philippians 4:4-7 from page 104
- a jug or bowl of water
- a jug of perfumed oil (not real chrism)
- an alb
- a large pillar candle, matches or lighter, and snuffer
- a small stand, such as a music stand, to hold the book during the ritual
- nourishing snacks for the break

Before the session

Prepare two areas as follows:

The Gathering Area
Arrange the seating as in previous sessions. Have on hand
- a name tag for each person
- a cross
- nourishing snacks for the break.

The Ritual Area
Arrange the seating as in previous sessions, and put the table and cloth in the centre of the space. On the cloth, place
- a Bible or lectionary with the duplicated pages inserted discreetly
- a jug or bowl of water
- a jug of perfumed oil (not chrism)
- an alb
- an unlit candle.

Leave room on the cloth for the cross.

Gathering

Greet the participants as they arrive and take them to the gathering space. Before you begin the session, distribute name tags and attend to any housekeeping matters.

Give participants a chance to share their responses from page 35, "The Light of Christ," and page 36, "Sharing the Light." If necessary provide the candidates with an opportunity to record answers in their books.

Introduce the session in words such as:

Today we are going to recall one of the final gestures in the rite of baptism. First, we are going to think about receiving messages. Think of the different ways we receive messages from friends, family or strangers.

Allow a moment of silence and then invite the participants to name different ways we receive messages. (For example: television, radio, telephone, e-mail, conversations, ads on TV or radio, words, looks on people's faces, feelings portrayed in photos and other art.)

Thank everyone and ask:

What do we need to do to receive a message? If someone sends us a letter, what do we need to do?

Invite responses.

Now ask:
How does someone special in your life make sure you get the message that they love you?

Allow for some silent reflection and then invite responses. (For example: words, a smile, a card, flowers, a special gift, time spent together, touching or holding you when you are upset or sad.) Then explore with the participants what they can do to make sure someone receives a message from them.

Conclude this discussion in words such as:

We are going to move to another space where we will pray and sing and recall words from the rite of baptism. Once again you will need to use all of your senses so that you may receive messages from God. It is important not to distract others.

Form the group into a procession. The adult who is not leading the ritual may invite one of the participants to carry the cross, lead the procession, and place the cross on the cloth when everyone is in place. The ritual leader should go last.

Ritual experience: awakened to grace

1. The group should end the procession around the table. Have the adult who is not leading the ritual light the candle.

2. Place the cross on the cloth.

3. When everything is ready, say:

On the day of your baptism you were claimed for Christ.
As you prepare to celebrate the sacrament of confirmation, the Christian community holds you in its heart Remember that God loves you.

Because you will be using the sign of the cross as part of the ritual experience, omit the usual sign of the cross greeting now.

4. Invite everyone to sit. Take the Bible from the cloth, and read the adapted text of Matthew 10:16-42. Because the session talks about many different ways to communicate, be sure to communicate your respect for the Word of God by standing with great dignity, holding the book graciously and reading very carefully. Then return the Bible to its place on the cloth.

5. After a few minutes of silence, say:

As we prepare to celebrate confirmation we enter again into the celebration of our baptism. On the day of our baptism after we received the lit candle, our ears and lips were touched and the Church, the people of God prayed:

The Lord Jesus made the deaf hear and the mute speak. May he soon touch your ears to receive his word, and your mouth to proclaim his faith, to the praise and glory of God.

6. Turn to the participant beside you and invite that person to stand. Trace the sign of the cross on both ears saying: *N., your ears have been opened by the grace of God. Hear the words of Christ.*

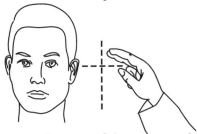

7. Then trace the sign of the cross on the lips saying :

N., your lips have been opened by the grace of God. Speak as Christ would speak. Profess the faith you hear for the glory of God.

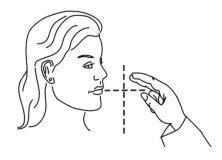

With a gesture, signal this person to remain standing.

Sing: **Blessed be God!**
All respond: **O blessed be God!**

8. Repeat each step with each participant. Be sure to include the other adult leader.

9. Once everyone has had a turn, gesture for everyone to sit.

10. Take the Bible from the cloth, and read the adapted text of Philippians 4:4-7. Because the session talks about many different ways to communicate, be sure to communicate your respect for the Word of God by standing with great dignity, holding the book graciously and reading very carefully

11. After a few moments of silence, gesture for everyone to stand. When all are standing, say:

Let us give thanks to God, always and for everything, in the name of our Lord Jesus Christ.

Sing: **Blessed be God!**
All respond: *O blessed be God!*

God our Father, we give you thanks for all your gifts so freely given to us.

Sing: **Blessed be God!**
All respond: *O blessed be God!*

For the beauty and wonder of your creation,in earth and sky and sea.

Sing: **Blessed be God!**
All respond: *O blessed be God!*

For all that is filled with your graces howing us the light of Christ.

Alive in the Spirit!
Leader's Guide **78**

Sing: **Blessed be God!**
All respond: *O blessed be God!*

**For minds to muse and hearts to love.
For hands to serveand health and
strength to work.**

Sing: **Blessed be God!**
All respond: *O blessed be God!*

**And above all, for the greatest gift given
to us: Christ Jesus our Lord. To him be
praise and glory with you and the Holy
Spirit, now and for ever.**

All respond: ***Amen.***

Getting in touch with the experience

At this point the two adult leaders
change roles. The ritual leader should
not lead the reflection and catechesis.

Call the group back to focus by singing
or saying: **Blessed be God!**
All respond: **O blessed be God!**

If necessary repeat two or three times.

Invite the participants to recall the
experience in words such as:

**Think about our conversation earlier
about receiving messages. Remember**

the passages we heard from the Bible.
Think about the gestures we used. We
prayed a prayer of thanksgiving.

Use the questions that follow to help
recall the ritual. Relax and allow for silence. Encourage everyone to respond,
but it is not necessary for everyone to
speak. Encourage the participants to go
beyond one-word answers. If they seem
reluctant, you may call on one of the
more outgoing members. For example
you can ask, **"What shape did N. trace
on your ears?" "What word did you
hear in the first reading?" "In the second reading?"** If they give brief answers,
invite more comments by asking, **"Can
you tell me more about that?"**

What did you hear?

Hoped-for responses
*scripture passages about being sent,
words about rejoicing, words about my
ears and lips being marked or opened,
the words "Blessed be God." Words
thanking God for music, hands, hearts
etc. People singing, people talking.
Silence. My name.*

What did you see?

Hoped-for responses
people standing and sitting, the sign of

*the cross being traced on other people, a
book, the oil, water, the cross, a candle*

What did you feel?

Hoped-for responses:
*the sign of the cross on my ears and lips,
uncomfortable when the leader signed
me, nervous not knowing what would
happen.*

Is there anything else you remember?

Hoped-for responses
Answers will vary.

Conclude by thanking everyone for their
participation. Extinguish the candle and
announce the break.

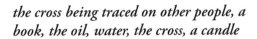

Catechesis on the experience

The session now moves from a reflection on the sensory nature of the experience to the catechesis based on the experience.

Phase 1
from the sensory experience of the ritual to hints about God

Phase 2
from God sending messages to us to our need to be opened to the grace of God

Phase 3
from the intent of baptism to my life in the Christian community

The questions and sample comments are offered as suggestions to encourage dialogue. Use the words of the participants and their responses to deepen the reflection and the catechesis.

Break
Offer everyone
a nourishing snack.

Phase 1

Initial Reflection on the Experience

In this first phase, you will rely mainly on the participants' insights. Assemble the group in the ritual area.
To call the group back to focus, sing or say: **Blessed be God!**
All respond: *O blessed be God!*

Invite everyone to sit silently and to recall the ritual actions. Highlight or recap their comments from before the break. Ask:

What messages did you receive in our celebration today?

Hoped-for responses
- God loves us.
- The community cares about us.
- We do not need to worry.
- God is sending us out.
- God wants us to rejoice.
- The cross is important because it was traced on us.
- God wants us to hear and to speak.

Remember there are no right or wrong answers. They may also comment on the items on the table or the other people. Ask:

Can you describe or explain how you received the message today? Was it in something someone said, or did, or something you saw?

Encourage the participants by repeating or rephrasing some of their responses. If they are hesitant, the adult who is not leading the catechesis could offer comments. You do not need to wait for a certain number of responses Ask:

Have you ever been somewhere and saw something that reminded you of God? Has something every happened that made you think about God?

The answers will vary. You may need to offer some examples such as a favourite animal or flower, lightning in the sky on a clear night, stars sparkling, someone helping a hurt person, images of war, pictures of children starving, beautiful music, stunning sunset, waves at the beach.

If the participants share "negative" images such as pictures of children starving or images of war, it is important to address these comments honestly. It is natural to wonder where God is during these difficult times. For young people it is challenging to understand that God is present in all of life's circumstances. God is not absent during the times of war or destruction. It is important to help the participants understand that God is with us in our pain, struggles and suffering. Sometimes it is possible to recognize God's presence in the actions of others in times of difficulty.

Thank everyone and summarize by commenting that God speaks to us in many different ways. God sends us messages through all things that God has created.

Phase 2

Connecting with Baptism

In this phase you do more of the talking. Remind everyone that at the time of their baptism the Christian community prayed that their ears would be opened to God. Acknowledge that sometimes it is easy, but often it can be difficult to hear God's messages. Ask:

Why do you think it can be difficult to recognize God's messages?

Hoped-for responses
We are busy doing other things, God's messages come through people, the message gets cut off or distorted (like the childhood game of "broken telephone").

Listen to their responses. Explain that God sends messages in different ways and through different people. Highlight that God sends messages through the

stories in the Bible. At Mass the homily is also a message from God. Prayers and hymns may also be messages from God. God does not rely on just one way to send messages. God also sends us messages through other people. Sometimes we know the people and other times we read or hear about the people and receive messages that way. Ask:

Why do you think the Church, the people of God, prayed that our ears would be opened to God when we were baptized?

Hoped-for responses
So we would be able to hear God's message.

Listen to their responses and then explain that God helps us to receive God's messages. Describe how when we are young our parents help us hear their messages by asking us to sit still or stop what we are doing so we can really listen. Our parents help us to receive the message. Explain that God makes it possible for us to receive messages. We need to be open to God. The Church touches our ears when we are baptized, but it is our whole lives that need to be open to God. We know that God gives us everything we have. God even gives us the ability to listen and to know God. (It can seem confusing that it is God who helps us to hear and to know God.)

Ask:

Why do you think the Church, the family of God, prayed that our lips would be opened and we would give glory to God when we were baptized?

Hoped-for responses
so we could tell others about God, so we could talk and share God's message.

Listen to their responses. Explain that we are to speak as Christ would speak. When Jesus spoke, he thanked his Father for all good things. Jesus talked to God about people in need and he talked to the people in need about God. We are called to do the same. We are to tell others about the great things God has done. We are to thank God for the great and wonderful things that have been done.

Explain that as Christians our first prayer is to offer praise and thanks for the marvellous things God has done. We need God's help to remind us to give thanks. Sometimes we pray to God when we need to ask for something. We also pray to God to say thank you for all the good things in our lives. It is the Spirit of God that helps us to pray both when we need something and when we need to thank God.

Continue by explaining that sometimes it may be a little confusing or we may be unsure about how we are to pray or what we need to say to God. God helps us at these times, too. Remind them of the reading from Matthew's gospel where God tells us not to worry about what we are to speak or say. God tells us that the Spirit will lead us. We can remember to begin our prayer by asking the Holy Spirit to help us pray.

Phase 3

My Life in the Christian Community

Conclude the above discussion by reminding the participants that as disciples of Jesus we have the Holy Spirit, our families and the parish to support us as we learn how to live the message that God has given us.

Remind everyone that God gives each of us the message that we are loved and important. This message is given in different ways. Each of us is asked to become for others this message of love.

One of our great heroes is St. Francis of Assisi. (You can ask them if they recall reading the prayer of St. Francis in their books.) Francis loved God very much and he taught his fellow believers to preach the gospel – to tell other people that God loves them. St. Francis said to preach the gospel and if necessary to use words. This is good advice for us.

We are to be a message to the world of God's love and care by the way we live. Sometimes we may need to use words to explain to others why we live this way. Ask:

How can you be a message from God to the world?

Listen to their answers. If necessary, encourage them to be more specific in their responses.

Conclude by explaining that we did not carry anything in the opening procession of this session because *they* are the message from God. They are the sign, the message of God's presence.

Connecting with confirmation and eucharist

Remind the participants that the Church uses seven gifts to describe the Holy Spirit. Point out that it is difficult to use just seven words to describe the Holy Spirit. Recall that in previous sessions we have spoken of the gifts of *understanding, wisdom, courage, right judgment, reverence* and *knowledge*. The seventh gift of the Holy Spirit is *wonder and awe in God's presence*. This gift helps us to be aware of God's presence and also helps us discover our total depen-

dence on God. The gift of wonder and awe in God's presence also helps us to hear God and profess our faith.

Explain that at the time of confirmation the entire Church prays that the gifts of the Holy Spirit will live in us and help us live as disciples of Jesus. On the day of confirmation as the minister of confirmation traces a cross on your head with the sacred chrism he will say, *"Be sealed with the Gift of the Holy Spirit."* You will say, *"Amen,"* and then he will say, *"Peace be with you."* Your response is, *"And also with you."* This brief dialogue is at the centre of the rite of confirmation. Confirmation is celebrated only once and eucharist is celebrated time and time again.

Explain that we are confirmed so that we can be full members of the family of God. Although our preparatory sessions are ending, our journey is not finished.

The gifts of the Holy Spirit will help us continue living as members of the family of God. As members of the family we gather each Sunday to celebrate the eucharist. We bring to this celebration the gift of our lives and the needs of our world. We praise and thank God for the gifts in our lives and, with the Christian community, we are strengthened by the body and blood of Jesus. Our journey continues Sunday after Sunday.

Bringing the session home

Ask the candidates to open their books to Session 5 on page 39. Remind them about the letter for their families on page 40. Explain that they should read pages 41 and 42, which are a summary of our time together.

Conclusion

Review the details of their upcoming celebration of the sacrament of confirmation.

Announce the date and time of confirmation and the session after confirmation, and ask the candidates to write this information in the space provided in the family letter.

Ask the candidates to turn to the prayers on pages 43 and 44 and invite them to pray these prayers each day with a member of their family. They could take turns leading the prayer. Together recite the prayer on page 44.

Before ending the session, remind the participants to take their personal belongings with them and to make sure that both the gathering space and ritual space are tidy. Finally, remind the candidates that you will see them for Session 6.

Session 6

Confirmed for Life

Note to the catechist

This session takes place after confirmation. There is no ritual experience because you will be recalling and reflecting upon the actual celebration of confirmation. It's important to schedule this gathering within a week of the celebration of confirmation.

This session allows for a larger group, so if you have had a number of smaller groups for the preparatory sessions, you may consider combining them. More adult leaders would be helpful for the latter part of the session; parents and sponsors are encouraged to participate in this session.

Session 6 consolidates the connections among confirmation, eucharist and daily living. In baptism we were established within the royal, priestly, prophetic family of God. In confirmation we are anointed with the Holy Spirit. In the weekly Sunday gathering of the Christian family we give praise and thanks for all God's gifts, we are nourished at the table of God's word, and we share the body and blood of Christ at the table of the eucharist. Then we are sent. The priest says, "Go in peace to love and serve the Lord." We don't just leave, like people who have all watched the same movie in a theatre. We are sent forth each week with something to do; we are apostles. The word *apostle* means "one who is sent."

This session begins with a mystagogical reflection on the celebration of confirmation. If a parish musician can be present, the reflection can include some of the liturgical music sung at the celebration. Music is one more way to surface memories of the celebration.

Most often confirmation is celebrated within eucharist. It is possible, however, to celebrate the sacrament within a liturgy of the Word. Although the sacrament is celebrated according to the rite, local parish or diocesan practices mean that each celebration will be unique. (In some dioceses, for example, the pastor is authorized by the bishop to confirm.) The notes for leading the mystagogical reflection because of these local differences need to be broad. This means that the leader's text is less detailed than it was for the five preparatory sessions.

This session is the sixth gathering – not the final event in the faith life of the newly confirmed. It is important to speak of future involvement in the life of the community and to remind the candidates that Sunday eucharist is the repeatable sacrament of initiation.

Preparing yourself

- Be sure you are familiar with the organization of the session and the words you will say.

- Decide who will lead the "getting in touch" activity before the break and who will lead the reflection and catechesis afterwards. You should share the work of leading the apostolic activity.

- Decide on the apostolic activity for the group.

Goals

Session 6 is intended to help the candidates:
- reflect on the experience of confirmation
- name ways of living as confirmed Christians
- participate in an apostolic activity.

Supplies and Environment

- a name tag for each person
- a chair, mat or cushion for each person
- a copy of the adapted text of Philippians 4: 4-7 from page 104 (already used in Session 5)
- a small table with a Bible or lectionary, with the adapted text discreetly inserted
- a jug of perfumed oil (not real chrism) if the oils are not displayed in the church
- a small table
- unconsecrated bread (the same type used at the celebration)
- some unconsecrated wine in a clear chalice or goblet.
- materials for your chosen apostolic activity (see sample list on page 95)
- nourishing snacks for the break

Before the session

The Parish Church

Place the Bible or lectionary on a small table in front of the ambo or lectern where the Word of God is normally read at Mass.

Place the unconsecrated bread and unconsecrated wine on a small table at the main communion station (usually in the centre aisle).

Place the jug of perfumed oil on a small table between the lectionary and the bread and wine.

(If the bishop led the confirmation, you may include his picture on the table.)

Have on hand
* a name tag for each person
* nourishing snacks for the break

The Catechetical Area

Arrange the seating as in previous sessions, and put the table and cloth in the centre of the space.
* Have pens and pencils on hand.
* Prepare supplies for the apostolic activity.

If the apostolic activity is being completed in a different space, prepare all materials in advance.

Gathering

Greet the participants as they arrive, distribute name tags, and invite them to gather in the main area at the front of the church.

Introduce the session in words such as:

Today we are going to reflect on the celebration of confirmation and focus on some ways that we are able to live as confirmed Christians.

Gesture for everyone to stand.

Sing or say: **Blessed be God!**
All respond: *O blessed be God!*

Say: **Let us pray.**

Pause for a moment of silent prayer.
Then continue:

**Ever-living God,
we praise you for all the gifts
you give to us.
We praise you for the gift of new life
received through the waters of baptism.
We thank you for the gift of the Holy
Spirit sent to be our guide and
companion.
We praise you for nourishing us with
the gift of Jesus' body and blood.
As we learn to live as confirmed
Christians may we always walk in harmony with the Holy Spirit.**

We pray in Jesus' name,
who lives and reigns with you
in the unity of the Holy Spirit,
one God forever and ever.

All respond: *Amen.*

Getting in touch with the experience of the sacrament

Invite everyone to sit. Speak slowly and deliberately and allow for a brief period of silence after each statement or question. (Although the text refers to the bishop, the pastor or perhaps a chancellor may have been the minister of confirmation. If present, the parish musician could play the music that was used during the celebration softly in the background.)

Allow for silence and then begin by explaining in these or similar words:

Today we are going to recall the celebration of confirmation. As I review the celebration, listen and allow your many different memories to surface. If it helps, close your eyes. Remember to keep a respectful silence and not to distract others.

Say:
Recall what happened at home just before you left for church. Remember who was present and what was going on.

Silence.

Ask:
When you arrived at the church, whom did you see? What were you feeling? Were there more people there than you expected? Was there anyone you were surprised to see?

Silence.

Ask:
What do you remember of the beginning of the celebration when Bishop N. (Father N.) first came in?

Silence.

Say:
We sat down.
(Then offer one or two lines from one of the readings or the gospel. The musician could sing the refrain from the psalm or the gospel acclamation.)

Ask:
What images do you recall from the Word of God?

Silence.

Ask:

When it came time for you to stand with your sponsor, how did you feel? What do you remember about the baptismal promises?

Silence.

Ask:

Do you remember how you felt when Bishop N. (Father N.) stretched out his hands and prayed for all the candidates? What words do you remember?

Silence.

Ask:

Can you recall how you felt when Bishop N. (Father N.) sealed you with chrism? Pause. **And then offered you the sign of peace?**

Silence.

Say:

You returned to your place and the liturgy continued. The bread and wine were brought forward. (This would be a good time for the parish musician to play.)

If eucharist was not celebrated, the reflection would move to the Lord's Prayer, blessing and dismissal.

Continue:

What words do you remember hearing about bread, wine, eating, drinking?

Silence.

Say:

Recall the communion procession, the people, the feelings you had, the song we sang.

Silence.

Ask:

What were the last words of the celebration? How did you feel leaving the celebration?

Silence.

Invite the participants to open their eyes and choose one word, image or memory from the celebration. Allow for a moment of silence and then ask the participants to simply raise their hands and you will invite them to speak. If others cannot hear the word, image or memory, repeat it.

Some of the other adult leaders may begin first. When the reflection is drawing to a close thank everyone for their participation and conclude this section by summarizing and articulating key catechetical points. Be sure to highlight the following:

- People gathered to celebrate confirmation with you because all sacraments are communal. We rely on each other to live as disciples.

- The Church reminds us that the sacraments are for all people – that is one reason that Bishop N. (or his representative, Father N.) celebrated with us.

- The Word of God guides us; we proclaim God's Word as part of every liturgy.

- Today your heads are no longer shiny from the chrism. However, you are still bright with the light of Christ. The way you live will be a sign of God's bright presence in your life.

Thank the participants for their participation and explain that after the break we will speak more about living as confirmed Christians. Then announce the break. Invite everyone to leave the church and gather in the catechetical area.

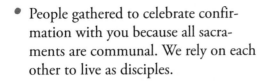

Break

Offer everyone
a nourishing snack.

Catechesis on living the sacraments

Invite the participants to come and sit in the catechetical area. At this point the leaders change roles. This section will provide an opportunity for the participants to share with others practical and concrete ways to live out confirmation at home, at work or school, and in the parish and community.

Call the group back to focus by singing or saying: **Blessed be God!**
All respond: *O blessed be God!*

Repeat two or three times if necessary.

Begin with a brief summary of the key points in the journey to confirmation. In these or similar words say:

On the day of baptism God gave you the gift of new life and welcomed you into the Christian family, the Church. During our sessions together we recalled that during baptism we were anointed, reminding us that we belong to God's royal family. The cross reminds us that we have received a new identity in baptism. Each time we sign ourselves with the cross we recall that we have put on Christ. We are called to reflect the light of Christ to the world. God opened our ears and our mouths so that we can proclaim the Good News to others.

Alive in the Spirit!
Leader's Guide **92**

Now you have been confirmed – anointed with the Holy Spirit. The Spirit will guide and support you in your life as a disciple.

The Christian community supports us as we try to live as disciples. That is one reason we gather each Sunday for eucharist with our parish family. We belong to God and to our parish family.

We are not baptized and confirmed for ourselves. We are baptized and confirmed so that we may live as confirmed Christians.

Ask:
How do confirmed Christians live?

Allow for responses.

Then continue by explaining that each time we gather to celebrate the eucharist we are dismissed. Ask if anyone can recall what is said to us at the end of eucharist.

Allow for responses.

If no one offers the correct answer remind them, **"Go in peace to love and serve the Lord."**

Continue by explaining that we do not just leave and go home the way we do after school or when a movie is ended.

We are sent from Mass with a job to do. God sends us into the world to be apostles. Jesus had many different apostles. Confirmed Christians are like Jesus' apostles. After confirmation Bishop N. (Father N.) sent us into the world do the work of apostles by loving and serving the Lord.

Say:
This work is so important that the Sunday eucharist is often called "the sending out" – except we don't use the English words "sending out," we use a word that comes from Latin, mass. I am sure that most often we use the word mass when we are talking about coming to church. When we call it the Mass we are saying that it is the gathering from which God sends our Christian family to do Christ's work in the world.

The priest says, *"Go in peace to love and serve the Lord."*
And we answer, *"Thanks be to God."*

Conclude with these words:
Our answer, *"Thanks be to God,"* helps us to remember St. Paul's words about living as Christians.

Take the Bible and read the adapted text of Philippians 4: 4-7.

Bringing the session home

Remind the participants that in previous sessions we talked about being light for the world and living as disciples. Explain that as fully initiated Christians they can continue some liturgical activities such as altar-serving, singing in the choir, or bringing the gifts of bread and wine to the table. Ask if they know of other ways they can be involved in the liturgy now that they are fully initiated. Invite responses.

If they do not mention the role of lector, cantor and minister of hospitality, be sure to explain that these roles are open to them as fully initiated members. (Note that it is important for the person to have the skill or gift to serve as a liturgical minister. For example, a lector needs to have the gift of proclamation, a cantor needs to be able to sing, and a minister of hospitality must be comfortable and at ease greeting others including people they don't know.)

Explain that for the remainder of the session we will explore ways to live our confirmation.

Invite the participants to sit in family groupings, so that three or four families can work together to share ideas if they choose to. If the family or sponsors are not present, ask the newly confirmed to form groups of four or five. The leaders can assist with forming groups and can also participate in one of the groups. Once the groups have formed and are ready to listen, invite them to think of the many different ways that they have already chosen to live like confirmed Christians at home, work or school, in the parish and the community.

You may find it helpful to provide some examples:

At home:
* sharing family chores
* gathering for family prayer

At school or work:
* walking away from others who want to gossip or tell mean-spirited jokes
* showing respect for people
* completing work in a conscientious way

In the parish:
* gathering for Sunday eucharist
* serving as a member of the choir, or as an altar server, etc.

In the community:
* helping at a food bank
* caring for a sick neighbour

Alive in the Spirit!
Leader's Guide **94**

Invite them to discuss their ideas in their groups. Once the discussion has begun invite them to turn to page 47 in their books, "Bringing Christ to the World," and write down some of their ideas under the heading What We Already Do.

When they have finished, invite them to discuss and make a list of other ways they can bring Christ to the world. After some discussion invite them to record one or two ideas that they would like to do under the heading What We Can Do In the Future.

Invite the participants to tidy up the work area and to prepare for the final activity.

Apostolic activity: bringing Christ into the world

Remind the participants that we love and serve the Lord by loving and serving others. Sometimes we care for those we know and other times we are called to care for people we don't know and may never even meet.

Explain that when we care for others and serve them as Jesus taught us we are doing apostolic work. Then name the apostolic activity you have chosen for the group. Explain what needs to be done and establish how the work will be finished. Parish circumstances and local situations need to be considered, so be daring and dream of different apostolic activities. Here are some examples:

- sort or stock food for the parish pantry

- make greeting cards for parish visitors to take to the infirm or nursing home residents

- plant flowers or seeds at the parish or a nearby school

- make a card of welcome to give to new parishioners or families preparing to celebrate baptism

- make thank-you cards for the parish prayer sponsors and others who assisted with the confirmation preparation

- sort clothing from a clothing drive

- clean up a local park or the parish property

- make placemats for use at a community meal such as Out of the Cold

- prepare cookies or muffins to be served at a parish social.

Conclusion

Clean and tidy the areas that have been used. Then gather the group for a final blessing and dismissal.

Thank everyone for participating and congratulate them for what has been accomplished in the apostolic activity. Invite the newly confirmed to show their families the letter in Session 6 (page 46).

Remind the newly confirmed that although the sessions are ended, our call to live as confirmed Christians continues. We live our confirmation for life.

Invite the participants to stand for the blessing. Remind the group to answer "Amen" to each part of this blessing:

Say:
We know that God has made us a family by water and the Holy Spirit: may God bless us and watch over us with abundant love.

All respond: *Amen.*

Say:
We believe that Jesus is Lord forever at the right hand of God: may we have the joy of knowing that he is also with us to the end of time.

All respond: *Amen.*

Say:
We know that the Holy Spirit has been poured into our hearts:may we use the Spirit's gifts to bring the joy of God's kingdom to the world.

All respond: *Amen.*

At this point everyone makes the sign of the cross, while saying:

In the name of the Father, the Son, and the Holy Spirit. Amen.

Then say:
Let us all go in peace to love and serve the Lord.

All respond: *Thanks be to God.*

A Sample Retreat

A retreat offers candidates – and family members who might also attend – an opportunity to get more deeply in touch with their own personal relationship with God. Activity levels vary throughout the retreat as does the degree and type of interaction with others. Full participation and engagement are important, but everyone should be assured that they will *never* be required to share their thoughts and feelings if they do not want to. Nor will anyone evaluate their work. For this reason each participant should be given a large envelope for storing their work; it will be a permanent remembrance of this retreat day.

Retreat Schedule

The best time for the retreat is after Session 5. The retreat may be long (4 hours) or short (2 hours). If the group is large you may consider establishing a station for each activity and have participants rotate through the stations in smaller groups. When you have a very large number of candidates you may consider offering the retreat on two or more occasions. See "Retreat Activities" for activity outlines.

Long Retreat *(4 hours)*

Opening Prayer

Activity A – Baking Bread
Break

Activity B – My God
or
Activity C – I Believe

Break

Activity D – Foot-washing Ritual

Bread Sharing

Short Retreat *(2 hours)*

Opening prayer

Activity B – My God
Break with snacks

Activity D – Foot-washing Ritual

This short retreat might be concluded with a sharing of tasty pre-baked bread. See #4–5 of the outline of Activity A – Baking Bread.

Retreat Activities

A. Baking Bread

Purpose: to allow participants to ponder the reason Christ and the Church use bread and share bread in the celebration of eucharist

Supplies
- an easy bread recipe
- ingredients for the bread recipe
- other equipment as outlined in the recipe
- an oven
- a cup of flour brought by each candidate
- extra flour for those who forget to bring their own
- butter and various jams and spreads

Outline

1. Invite the candidates to add their flour to the large bowl in which the bread dough will be mixed.

2. Finish mixing the ingredients according to the recipe. Be sure to allow each of the candidates a turn to help with the mixing.

3. Bake the bread and set it aside for eating at the end of the retreat.

4. At the end of the retreat, gather the group to share the bread, adding to it their choice of butter, jam or other spread. Say a blessing before eating. After sharing the bread, bring the group to silence and comment that we are like the wheat and flour used to make the bread. The flour from many seeds is mixed together and changed into bread to feed us. At eucharist, as we all share the bread of life, God unites us with each other and with Christ and makes us into "food" for the life of the world.

5. Invite participants to briefly recall how we can be food for the world.

B. My God

Purpose: to allow participants to ponder their image of God

Supplies
a copy of one of the following, all of which address the concept of forming an image based on our experience:

   –any version of the Indian folktale "The Blind Men and the Elephant" (readily available on the internet and in bookstores)
   –a variety of passages from scripture that describe God; for example: Psalm 18: 1-3. Psalm 18: 28, Psalm 23, Psalm 27: 1, Psalm 29, and Psalm 62:7
   –*Old Turtle* by Douglas Wood (Pfiefer-Hamilton Publishers, 1992)

Alive in the Spirit!
Leader's Guide **98**

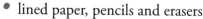

- lined paper, pencils and erasers
- art materials
- copies of photographs or drawings of nature, people, animals

Outline

1. Before starting to read the psalms or story aloud
- draw attention to the fact that in the selection someone will say that God is like something they know
- for "The Blind Men and the Elephant," tell them to listen and think about how the elephant is like God
- if you have chosen to read passages from scripture, before you begin explain that the verses are taken from different psalms.

2. Ask the group to listen carefully to the different ways God is described as you read the psalms or story aloud

3. When you have finished reading, invite the group to sit briefly in silence before speaking. Then briefly discuss what they have heard.

4. Point out that our own idea of God has grown inside us throughout our life, and will continue to grow and change. We will have learned about God from things that happen at home, at church, and out in the world of friends and of nature; and from people we meet—our family, priests, and maybe even teachers.

5. Invite participants to reflect in silence on some questions about God.

What in this world is most like God?
(A certain animal, a certain person, a certain plant, a part of the earth or the universe)
Anything else? Why?
How are you like God?
How are you different from God?

Allow lots of time for thought after each question.

6. Explain that now everyone will have a chance to do something to record the image of God they have thought about today. Show them the lined paper and pencils, the art materials, and the photographs or drawings and tell them that they may choose from among the materials to record their thoughts: in writing, in poetry or in art.

Candidates who are not able to record their thoughts by writing or drawing may be assisted by a trusted adult acting as secretary. Alternatively, you may supply a tape recorder and a private space in which they can record their spoken thoughts.

7. Tell participants that this is to be their own work. They may help another with spelling if asked, but they should not

comment on what they see others doing. You may ask them to work in silence if it seems appropriate for the group.

8. Conclude the activity by praying together the Lord's Prayer or Psalm 23 as found in their book.

C. I Believe

Purpose: to allow participants to think about their deepest beliefs

Supplies
a copy of one of the following, all of which address the concept of firmly held beliefs:
* any version of the Indian folktale "The Blind men and Elephant" (readily available in bookstores)
* "The Sneetches" from *The Sneetches and Other Stories* by Dr. Seuss (Random House, 1976)
* *Old Turtle and the Broken Truth* by Douglas Wood (Scholastic Press, 2003)
* *Old Turtle* by Douglas Wood (Pfiefer-Hamilton Publishers, 1992)

Outline
1. Gather the participants and read the story aloud.

2. Invite everyone to reflect on what they believe to be true.

3. Distribute paper and pencils. Allow time for participants to make a list of 5–10 things they deeply believe.

4. To conclude, distribute copies of the Apostles' Creed and recite it together.

D. Foot-washing Ritual

Purpose: to allow participants to ponder Christ's command to love others

Supplies
* a Bible or lectionary with the adapted text of John 13:1-15 (see page 105) inserted discreetly
* water
* basins and jugs
* a small towel brought by each candidate
* extra towels for those who forget to bring their own

Outline
1. Gather the participants around a basin and jug of water. Each person should have their towel at their place.

2. Remove your shoes and socks and then invite everyone else to remove theirs too.

3. When everyone has settled, ask someone to take the Bible and read the adapted text of John 13:1-15.

4. Immediately after the reading, quietly and without comment begin ritually to wash the feet of each one and dry them with a towel. Calm instrumental music may be played if you wish, but a respectful silence should be maintained.

5. Invite the last person to wash your feet. Then say:

Jesus said, *"You do not understand now what I am doing, but later you will understand. You call me Teacher and Lord – and you are right, for that is what I am. So if I, your Lord and Teacher, have washed your feet, you also ought to wash one another's feet. For I have set you an example, that you also should do as I have done to you."*

Pause in silence for a brief time.

6. Ask:

How did it feel to take off your shoes and socks today? Why?

How did you feel while you were waiting for your turn?

How did it feel to have your feet washed today?

When everyone has had a chance to speak, share your own feelings about washing all their feet.

7. Conclude by saying:

We call Jesus Teacher and Lord. If he, our Lord and Teacher, washed the feet of his friends, we also ought to wash one another's feet. For he has set you an example, that we also should do as he has done to us. He has given us a new commandment: love one another as he has loved us.

Reproducible Pages

Adapted scripture passage for session 1

There was an important man named Nicodemus

who came to Jesus and said to him,

"I know you have come from God,

for no one can do what you do

without God."

Jesus answered him,

"Yes, and no one can live in the kingdom of God

without being born again of water and the Spirit.

God loves the world so much that he sent me

so that all who believe will live forever."

John 3:1-16

Adapted scripture passage for session 3

As many of you as were baptized into Christ

have clothed yourselves with Christ.

All of you are one in Christ Jesus.

Let the same mind be in you

that was in Christ Jesus.

Galatians 3:27, 28b and Philippians 2:5

Adapted scripture passages for session 5

I am sending you out into the world; so be wise.

Do not worry about how you are to speak

or what you are to say;

for what you are to say will be given to you at that time.

For it is not you who speaks,

but the Spirit of your Father speaking through you.

What I say to you in the dark, tell in the light;

and what you hear whispered,

proclaim from the housetops.

Matthew 10:16-42

Rejoice in the Lord always;

again I say, Rejoice.

The Lord is near.

Do not worry about anything,

but in everything by prayer with thanksgiving

let your needs be made known to God.

And the peace that is so deep we can never understand it

will guard your hearts and your minds in Christ Jesus.

Philippians 4:4-7

Adapted scripture passage for the retreat foot-washing ritual

When Jesus knew that his time had come to go to the Father,

he gathered his disciples.

During supper Jesus got up from the table,

took off his robe, and tied a towel around himself.

Then Jesus said to them,

"You do not understand now what I am doing,

but later you will understand."

Then he poured water into a basin

and began to wash the disciples' feet

and to wipe them with the towel that was tied around him.

After he had washed their feet, he put on his robe

and returned to the table.

Then he said to them,

"Do you know what I have done to you?

You call me Teacher and Lord— and you are right, for that is what I am.

So if I, your Lord and Teacher, have washed your feet,

you also ought to wash one another's feet.

For I have set you an example,

that you also should do as I have done to you."

John 13:1-15

How is Confirmation Celebrated?

Confirmation may be celebrated within Mass or outside Mass. Even when eucharist is not included, the celebration always begins with the liturgy of the word. The bishop is the usual minister of the sacrament, but he may give parish priests permission to administer the sacrament in his place or with him.

Liturgy of the word

If confirmation is celebrated at a Sunday Mass, the Sunday readings are used. If confirmation is celebrated at another time, the parish may choose from a large and rich selection of readings for celebrating confirmation. If you wish to study or pray with the readings to be used in your child's celebration, your parish priest can help you find them.

Presentation of the candidates

The celebration begins to focus on confirmation right after the gospel. Someone from the parish presents the candidates; if the group is not too large their names may be announced. The candidates may be asked to come forward at this time or they may remain in their seats until later. When the candidates do come forward, their sponsors accompany them.

Homily or instruction

The bishop (or priest) then gives a brief homily. Sometimes this takes the form of a dialogue with the candidates.

Renewal of baptismal promises

After the homily, the candidates are asked to renew their baptismal promises. They might remember doing this at the Easter Vigil, at Easter Sunday Mass, or when infants are baptized at a regular Sunday Mass. It is done here to highlight the link between baptism and confirmation (and eucharist). If they are not already standing, the candidates will be asked to stand. Together the candidates answer "I do" confidently to each question.

Laying on of hands

The bishop (or priest) then invites everyone present to pray with him on behalf of the candidates and everyone prays silently for a short period of time. Then he and any other priests who will help him to administer the sacrament extend their hands over the group and pray for them. The prayer asks the Holy Spirit to guide the candidates and asks for seven special spiritual gifts.

Anointing with chrism

Next, the sponsor places their right hand on their candidate's right shoulder and tells the bishop the candidate's name (or the candidates may say their own names). Candidates for confirmation now use only their baptismal name (the Church has ceased the practice of having candidates take a confirmation name).

The bishop (or priest) then anoints the candidates. He dips his right thumb in the chrism and makes the sign of the cross on the candidate's forehead. (Some pour oil on the candidate's head and rub it in, finishing by making the sign of the cross with the right thumb on the forehead.)

While he is doing this he says the candidate's name and then, "Be sealed with the Gift of the Holy Spirit." The candidate answers, "Amen."

Sign of peace

Finally, the bishop (or priest) says the words that Jesus said to his disciples the first time he saw them after he rose from the dead, when he breathed on them and bestowed the Holy Spirit on them, saying, "Peace be with you." The candidate answers, "And also with you." Unlike Sunday Mass, there is usually no handshake or other action at this time because of the chrism on the bishop's hands.

The candidates will be instructed when to return to their seats.

General intercessions

The community then prays for the needs of the candidates and of the world using the same form as at Sunday Mass.

Liturgy of the eucharist

The liturgy of the eucharist begins. Some of the candidates may be asked to bring the gifts of bread and wine to the altar. At communion time the candidates receive communion first; they may receive under both kinds.

Outside Mass

If the sacrament is not celebrated within Mass, the celebration concludes with the Lord's Prayer and a blessing or prayer. The people are then dismissed.

Questions Families Often Ask

What are the requirements for a sponsor?

Each candidate for confirmation is to be accompanied by a sponsor. If possible, the godparent from baptism is encouraged to serve as sponsor. The sponsor should be a Catholic who is at least sixteen years old, has already been confirmed, has received the eucharist, and is living a life of faith. The sponsor is meant to be a role model and mentor for the candidate. A parent may not serve as a sponsor. (See Canons 892, 893, 874§3.)

Do candidates choose a confirmation name?

Candidates are always confirmed with their baptismal name. It is not necessary for them to choose an additional name.

Is there special clothing for confirmation candidates?

Since an alb is the garment of the baptized, it has become customary in some parishes for candidates to wear white gowns. This is not necessary; candidates may simply wear their "Sunday best."

In the past candidates have sometimes been asked to make a stole. Because a stole is a symbol of ordination, it is a garment worn by a deacon, priest or bishop. It is inappropriate for confirmation candidates to wear stoles.

Are candidates for confirmation required to celebrate the sacrament of reconciliation?

Candidates for confirmation have the same responsibilities as all Catholics. As explained in Canon 988, they are bound to confess grave sins, and are also encouraged to confess venial sins. If a candidate for confirmation has never celebrated the sacrament of reconciliation, an invitation to prepare for and celebrate the sacrament is extended, but the Church may not and does not keep a record of those who celebrate the sacrament of reconciliation.

Word List

Words in italics appear in the glossary as main entries.

Anoint: to rub or pour oil on someone or something. The Church uses three holy oils: the oil of the sick, the oil of catechumens, and *chrism*. The anointing of the sick is for comfort, healing and strength in time of suffering. The anointing of catechumens is for strengthening throughout the period of the catechumenate. The use of chrism is described below.

Baptism: the first *sacrament* of *Christian initiation*. Candidates are immersed in water or water is poured on them in the name of the Trinity. In baptism we share in Christ's dying and rising and experience a new birth as children of God. By this sacrament we are eternally joined to Christ and his Church.

Baptismal Candle: the candle presented to newly baptized persons during the celebration of *baptism*. It is a reminder that in baptism we receive the light of Christ, our faith is awakened, and we have Christ and the Spirit as our guides.

Baptismal Garment: the white clothing worn by newly baptized persons. At a celebration of infant *baptism* it is usually a long gown, but sometimes, particularly for boys, it is a white suit. In the unusual situation where the baby does not have a white garment, the minister of baptism simply touches the baby with a piece of white cloth. The baptismal garment is a reminder that the baptized person has been clothed in Christ and is a new person. Another example of a baptismal garment is the alb, a large white gown that covers the entire body. Priests and deacons always wear albs at Mass under the coloured vestments. In fact, all baptized people are entitled to wear albs at liturgical celebrations.

Baptismal Font: the pool or large bowl of holy water in every parish church in which *baptism* is celebrated.

Chrism (KRIZ-um): the special perfumed oil that is blessed by the bishop each year just before Easter. The Church uses chrism in four *anointings:* in the celebration of the *baptism* of someone who will not be confirmed immediately, in the celebration of the *sacrament* of *confirmation,* in the celebration of the sacrament of holy orders (ordination), and in the anointing of the church walls and the altar when a new church or altar is first used.

Christian Initiation: the process by which we become Christian. It involves the celebration of three sacraments:

baptism, confirmation and *eucharist*. In the sacraments of initiation a person is made one with Christ, made to be like him. When an adult is initiated, the Church celebrates all three in one celebration after a period of apprenticeship and preparation. In the Roman Catholic Church children baptized as babies are brought to the other two sacraments of Christian initiation at a time when they are able to be personally prepared.

Confirmation: the second *sacrament of Christian initiation*. Candidates are anointed on the forehead with *chrism*. In confirmation we share in Christ's exaltation as Spirit-filled Lord of glory and are strengthened by the Holy Spirit to share in Christ's work in the world.

Ephphetha (EFF-uh-thuh): the part of the celebration of *baptism* in which the candidates' ears and mouths are touched and the Church prays that the newly baptized may profess the faith they hear. The name of this ritual is taken from the word spoken by Jesus when he cured a man who could not hear or speak. It means "Be opened." The ephphetha rite draws our attention to our total dependence on God.

Eucharist: the third and only repeatable *sacrament* of *Christian initiation*, often called "Mass" or "communion." At each celebration of the eucharist, the faithful share in the body and blood of Christ under the form of bread and wine, which are consecrated during the eucharistic prayer. In eucharist we celebrate with Christ at the table of the Lamb of God, a foretaste of the heavenly banquet feasting on the food of eternal life. Participation in this sacrament nourishes lifelong growth in Christ.

Gifts of the Holy Spirit: wisdom, understanding, right judgment (counsel), courage (fortitude), knowledge, reverence (piety), and wonder and awe in God's presence (fear of the Lord).

Holy Oils: the oils blessed by the bishop each year just before Easter. In each parish church the holy oils are stored in their containers, called stocks, in a special cupboard called the ambry. In some churches the oils are displayed in a public part of the building; in others, mostly older churches, the ambry may not be in a public place. The Church uses three holy oils: the oil of the sick, the oil of catechumens, and *chrism*. The oil of the sick is for comfort, healing and strength in time of suffering. The oil of catechumens is for strengthening throughout the period of the catechumenate. The use of chrism is described above.

Holy Water Stoup: the small bowl of holy water at the entry to the church. It may be attached to a wall or placed on a stand.

Paschal Candle: the large candle that is blessed and lit for the first time at the Easter Vigil each year. It is a reminder of Christ, the light of the world, and is usually the largest candle in the church building. The paschal candle is generally kept near the *baptismal font.* It is lit for all liturgical celebrations during the 50 days of the Easter season, at all baptisms and for all funeral liturgies.

Sacrament: a celebration by Christ and his Church that uses words and actions (outward signs) to reveal the action of God in the life of the candidate. These actions include: the water bath of *baptism*, the *anointings* at *confirmation* and ordination, the anointing of the sick, the *eucharistic* feast (and the reserved consecrated bread), the exchange of marital vows, and the reconciling laying of hands on sinners.

Sponsor: the mentor, role model and companion who accompanies the *confirmation* candidate. If possible, the godparent from *baptism* is encouraged to serve as sponsor. The sponsor should be a Catholic who is at least sixteen years old, has already been confirmed, has received the *eucharist*, and is living a life of faith. A parent may not serve as a sponsor. (See Canons 892, 893, 874§3.) During the celebration of confirmation, the sponsor places their right hand on the candidate's right shoulder and may tell the bishop the candidate's name.

NOTES

NOTES

NOTES

NOTES

NOTES